the
Guitarist's Guide
to the Capo

First published in 2003 by Artemis Editions

An imprint of Artemis Music Limited
Pinewood Studios, Pinewood Road, Iver Heath,
Buckinghamshire SL0 0NH

This work © Copyright Artemis Music Limited 2003

ISBN: 0-634-06744-3

From an original idea by Andrew King

Project editor: James Sleigh
Book design and layout: Fresh Lemon
Photography: Darrin Jenkins
Music setting: Digital Music Art
CD audio: Martin Shellard

Artemis | EDITIONS
www.artemismusic.com

the Guitarist's Guide
to the Capo

by Rikky Rooksby

Artemis | EDITIONS

contents

preface

If you own a guitar the chances are that you have a small plastic or metal device stuffed into a pocket in your guitar case, or dropped behind the hi-fi where it lies gathering dust. To the untrained eye it looks like a plastic replica jawbone of a small prehistoric reptile, a medieval instrument of torture, or perhaps a new type of heavy metal armband. But this neglected piece of guitar hardware is, in fact, a *capo tasto* (or 'capo' for short) and it's possibly the single most interesting piece of kit you can buy for your guitar.

The capo is quite simply one of the most useful devices ever invented for guitarists. It doesn't run on batteries, it doesn't need a mains supply, and it will fit in your pocket. With this gadget you can play authentic versions of other people's songs, find the key that suits your voice, find new chords and new inspiration, and get new tones from your guitar.

This book is the most in-depth look at the humble capo ever published – it's nothing less than a complete user's guide to this most essential bit of guitarist's paraphernalia. It will tell you everything you ever wanted to know about the capo, including its history, design, construction, drawbacks, benefits, and the musical uses to which one can be put. It will tell you the best type of capo for you, and help you get the most out of it once you've parted with your hard-earned cash.

There are musical examples for you to try out and easy reference diagrams to show how to transpose a song into a better key, and how to tell what chords you are playing when you have a capo at the 5th fret. There's even a list of famous songs which need a capo to be played properly.

If you don't own a capo, buy this book first and get all the inside information you need.

If you do have one, this book will have you clamping your way to guitar heaven!

Rikky Rooksby

about the author

Rikky Rooksby is a guitar teacher, songwriter/composer, and writer on popular music. He is the author of *How To Write Songs On Guitar* (2000), *Inside Classic Rock Tracks* (2001), *Riffs* (2002), *The Songwriter's Sourcebook* (2003), and contributed to *Classic Guitars Of The Fifties*, *Guitar: A Complete Guide For The Player* (Balafon 2002) and *Roadhouse Blues: Stevie Ray Vaughan and Texas R'n'B* (Backbeat 2003).

He has written a number of articles on rock musicians for the new Dictionary Of National Biography (OUP), and published interviews, reviews, articles and transcriptions in magazines such as *Guitar Techniques, Total Guitar, Guitarist, Bassist, The Band, Record Collector, Music Collector, Encore, Sound On Sound*, and *Making Music* where for many years he wrote the monthly 'Private Pluck' guitar column. He is a member of the Guild of International Songwriters and Composers and the Vaughan Williams Society.
Visit his website at **rikkyrooksby.com**.

how to read chord diagrams

As we explore the fascinating new musical worlds that a capo opens up, you'll get the chance to play through some great-sounding chord sequences. There's no need to read musical notation as all the musical examples are described using chord fretbox diagrams. Here's how they work:

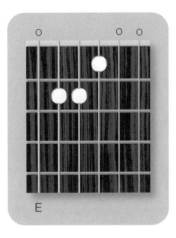

The diagram represents the neck of your guitar, as if you were looking straight on at the fretboard. The vertical lines on the diagram represent the six strings of the guitar, with the low E string on the left (the thickest string) and the high E string on the right (the thinnest string). The horizontal lines represent the frets, with the top of the diagram representing the nut of your guitar.

Each 'blob' represents a finger. An 'o' above a string represents an open (i.e. unfretted) string, while an 'x' shows a string that shouldn't be struck.

Chord diagrams further up the neck look like this:

Notice that the thick 'nut' at the top of the diagram has disappeared and is now the same thickness as all the other frets. The fret at which the shape is to be played is shown clearly by the side of the diagram.

The curved line joining the blobs at the fifth fret indicates a barre - in this case, it's telling you to use your first finger to hold down all the strings at the fifth fret. Barres don't always stretch across all six strings - the length of the curved line will tell you how many strings to hold down. Fortunately, one of the main advantages of the capo is that it enables you to avoid playing barre chords, so you won't find too many of them in this book!

Throughout this book, chords are named according to their shapes. So, for example the chord shape of E shown on this page will always be labelled as E, even if you have a capo at the fifth fret and the actual sounding chord is A. Similarly, the fret markings always refer to the distance from the capo, not from the nut. In cases where a guitar is capoed, the nut on the chord diagram represents the position of the capo.

The only exception to these rules is the case of partial capos, where all the fret positions and chord names are absolute, and refer to the uncapoed guitar. These cases are clearly marked in the text where they occur.

When strings are referred to in the text, they are numbered from 1 to 6, with 1 being the highest and 6 the lowest.

how I learned to stop worrying and love the capo

"A 'capo' should only be used by those who find that pieces of music are written too low for them to comfortably sing while playing."

J.Sampson's *Specialized Course of Guitar Lessons* (1946)

Readers of the above book could be forgiven for thinking that a capo was somehow a less than respectable device for a guitarist to be seen using. To this day, capos are thought of as a being bit of a cheat, in the same way that some people have very conservative views about guitar tunings.

I once took an acoustic guitar into a music shop to have some adjustments made. I was writing songs at that time in altered tunings and the guitar was in open D. I was curtly informed that the guitar was meant to be played in EADGBE, as though this were the 11th commandment. Of course, as all enlightened guitarists now know, altered tunings open up a whole new world of sonic possibilities for the adventurous musician, and the same is true of the humble capo.

Barre chords can be tricky for beginners...

Capos are considered a cheat because they enable you to play in keys that would normally require a barre chord. As many a beginner guitarist has found to their cost, the finger strength required to hold down a barre is often difficult to develop, and hence those players who resorted to a capo to get round the problem were looked down on by their more accomplished colleagues.

However, irrespective of the technical challenges involved, using a capo simply creates a totally different sound to playing barre shapes. The use of open strings creates a more vibrant, ringing tone that can't be reproduced when all six strings are being fretted. Not only that, but because all your fingers are involved in holding down the barre shape, you won't be free to add the embellishments typical of finger-picking styles.

Try playing this tune through, firstly with the top set of barre chord shapes (as demonstrated on **Track 1**) and then with the capo at the fifth fret and the bottom set of open chord shapes. Check out **Track 2** to hear the different sound that is created:

...but can be avoided with a capo!

No capo

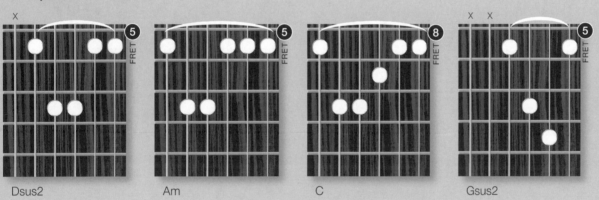

Dsus2   Am   C   Gsus2

Capo at 5th fret

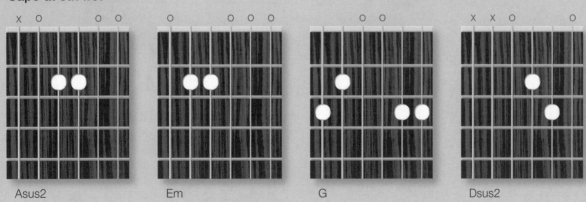

Asus2   Em   G   Dsus2

Listen out for the passing notes and other embellishments that can be included in the capoed version, because the fretting hand has sufficient free fingers to play them.

a brief history of the capo

The capo's full name is *Capo tasto*, an Italian term – *capo* means 'head' and *tasto* means 'tie'. The French term is, confusingly, *barre*, while the German is *capodaster*.

According to the *New Grove Encyclopaedia Of Music* the term's first recorded printed use was by G.B. Doni in his book *Annotazioni* (1640). The term *capo tasto* is recorded in Stainer and Barrett's *Dictionary of Musical Terms* (1876) and the *Grove Dictionary of Music* (1879), and *capodastros* appear on the *Army and Navy Co-Op Society Price List* in 1897.

So, the capo seems to have been around for at least four hundred years and was probably invented to allow musicians to play fretted instruments in various keys while maintaining easy and familiar fingering patterns – very much the same reason that most people use it today.

Two of the earliest designs featured a screw that would fix the capo at the back of the neck and Flamenco guitarists still use a capo based on a wooden design called the *cejilla*, invented toward the end of the eighteenth century. Capos were also designed for related instruments such as the banjo and mandolin.

According to research carried out by the Capo Museum (currently residing at w1.865.telia.com/~u86505074/capomuseum/), James Ashborn of Connecticut applied for the first American capo patent in 1850. Since then a plethora of designs have been introduced, with the most durable being the elastic capo (patented by W. H. Russell in 1931) and the first plastic capo (invented by H. Bauerfeind in 1973).

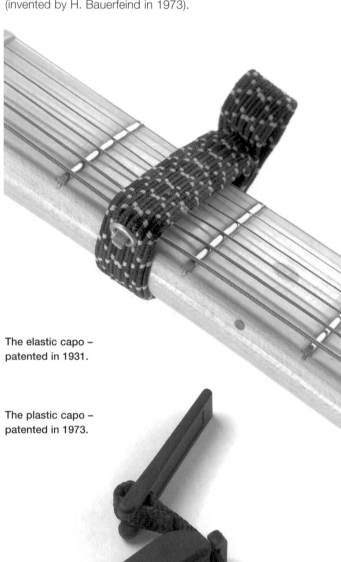

The elastic capo – patented in 1931.

The plastic capo – patented in 1973.

The *cejilla* – a wooden and leather device used by flamenco guitarists.

Since its invention in 1931 the elasticated capo (as shown on p. 10) has been the cheapest and most widely available capo. It was later superceded by metal clamp-like capos which almost always needed to be squeezed against the neck to ensure that all the strings were sounding, and could make the guitar neck-heavy.

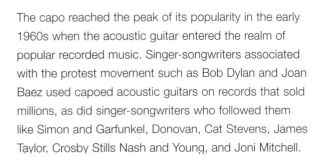

A Wittner capo featuring a heavy 'gate-latch' mechanism.

The capo reached the peak of its popularity in the early 1960s when the acoustic guitar entered the realm of popular recorded music. Singer-songwriters associated with the protest movement such as Bob Dylan and Joan Baez used capoed acoustic guitars on records that sold millions, as did singer-songwriters who followed them like Simon and Garfunkel, Donovan, Cat Stevens, James Taylor, Crosby Stills Nash and Young, and Joni Mitchell.

For a solo performer it was vital to vary the key of songs to add some tonal variation and the capo provided an easy way to do that, especially if your knowledge of chords was rudimentary. In addition, guitarists such as John Renbourn, Bert Jansch (both of whom played in the successful group *Pentangle*), Leo Kottke, and Nick Drake took acoustic playing to new heights, often involving the use of the capo. Since the 1960s the capo has been a permanent fixture of guitar technique in many styles of music.

The turning point in modern capo design came in 1978 when R. Shubb improved the C-clamp idea by adding a screw at the back, allowing the tightness of the clamping mechanism to be adjusted.

Since the 1970s capo design has improved steadily and today there are hundreds of patented designs that all aim to clamp the strings of the guitar evenly (effectively replacing the nut), allowing all six strings to ring clearly. The most common types of capo are surveyed below.

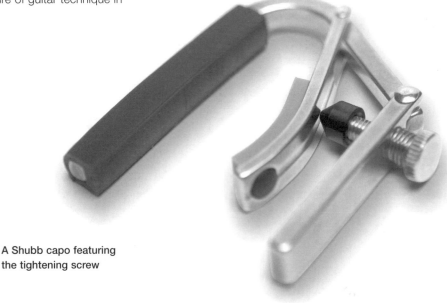

A Shubb capo featuring the tightening screw

a survey of capo models

Although the purchase of a capo is perhaps not worthy of as much heartache and consideration as investing in a new guitar, there are still some basic questions you should ask yourself before parting with any money:

How wide is your guitar neck?

If you want to use a capo with a 12-string or Spanish nylon-strung guitar make sure that the capo can cope with the wider neck.

How obtrusive do you mind it being?

This is partly an aesthetic consideration but also a practical one – a bulky or oddly shaped capo can easily catch on leads or other obstructions, and one that inhibits your playing will quickly become irritating. Make sure that you take the time to really put each capo through its paces in your local music store before you part with any cash.

How quick a change do you need to make?

Some capos are specifically designed to allow very quick changes of capo position. For example, if you play a song that modulates halfway through, do you want to be able to re-capo at a different fret mid-song?

Is your guitar neck flat or curved?

Most capos will fit most necks but a pronounced curve will mean a straight capo won't make good contact with the top and bottom Es at the same time.

How critical is tuning stability?

There's nothing more irritating (for the rest of the band and for the audience) than a guitarist who needs to retune for every single song because he's changed to a different capo position. If you're planning to use your capo in live performance then it may be worth spending a bit extra.

The Glider capo allows lightning fast changes of position.

1. the elastic capo (Bill Russell model)

This popular design is cheap and very light, and was one of the earliest mass-marketed capos. It consists of a metal bar sheathed in plastic. Either end of the bar goes through an 'eye' into a length of durable elasticated material.

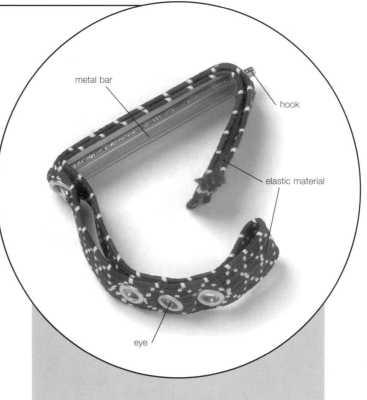

metal bar

hook

elastic material

eye

One end of the elasticated material has several 'eyes', spaced a short distance apart. The bar is placed at the desired fret, the material is then stretched round the back of the neck and hooks on through one of the holes.

capo tips

Over a period of time the elastic can fray.
Care must be taken during gigs – one false slip with that elastic and your capo will land in someone's drink at the back of the room!

also available

Similar capos are made by JHS (Curved Elastic Capo) and Jim Dunlop.

in brief

A good entry-level capo.

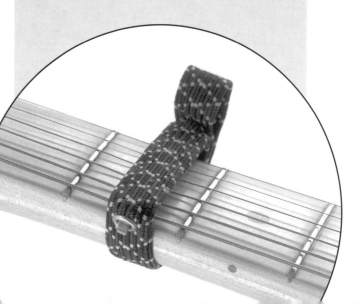

2. the Jim Dunlop 'lever action' capo

This slightly more sophisticated capo uses a curved rubber piece to hold the strings – affixed to the back of this rubber strip is a metal fixing mechanism with four notches. A length of non-elastic material goes round the neck and the plastic lever at the end of it fixes in between the teeth.

The lever is then pushed flat causing the capo to lock into position and exert pressure.

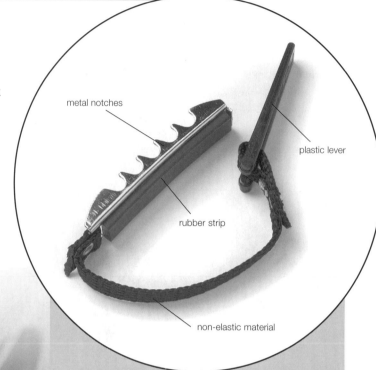

metal notches

plastic lever

rubber strip

non-elastic material

capo tips

Light and cheap and won't wear a hole in your jacket pocket.

Try to prevent the capo sliding sideways as you push the lever down, which in turn would drag the strings out of position.

Very quick to take off.

The material may need minor adjustment to fit round the neck as it is not elasticated.

also available

Terry Gould also make a capo of this type – the UGC8.

in brief

Another good entry-level capo.

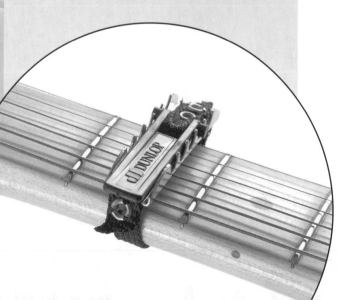

3. the Jim Dunlop c-clamp capo

An popular variation on this design from the 1960s was known as the *Hamilton* capo – a heavy, bulky design, it featured a bar that swung across to lock into position and didn't always make an effective grip on the neck. Jim Dunlop's C-Clamp is lighter and neater and doesn't unbalance your guitar neck. Its relatively small size means that it can be positioned close to the fret without it feeling as though your fretting hand is always in danger of bumping into it.

The lower 'jaw' moves to fit the angle of the neck. The capo is tightened by turning the screw against this lower jaw.

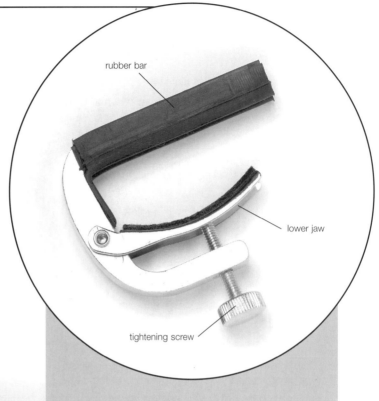

rubber bar

lower jaw

tightening screw

capo tips

Compared to the lever action model this capo takes longer to fit – unscrewing the capo from one position, moving it to a new position and tightening it could easily take 10 seconds.

in brief

A reliable and modestly priced capo.

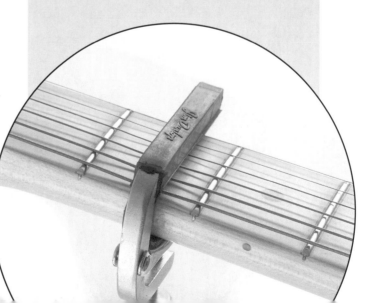

4. the Shubb 'original' capo

Shubb impressed many guitarists when they first launched their capos. Here was a company that took the whole business seriously.

The Shubb Original comes in a fetching gold finish, is 2" wide and has a slight curve. In addition to the fixed rubber-coated arm which holds the strings, there are two lower 'jaws'. The middle one has a smaller piece of gray rubber to protect the wood of the neck. Below that is a second moveable arm into which is inserted a screw/spring with a rubberized tip to exert pressure on the middle jaw and thus improve the force of the locking action. Shubb call this the "over-center locking action".

This gives an excellent, immediate setting of the capo, which tends to leave the strings in the correct alignment. A simple pull on the lever and the capo lifts away.

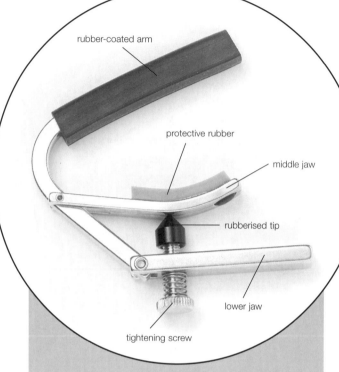

rubber-coated arm

protective rubber

middle jaw

rubberised tip

lower jaw

tightening screw

capo tips

Careful setting of the screw will allow the capo to lock firmly to the neck in any position but will not exert any more pressure than is needed to get clean notes. This prevents the strings from being pushed out of tune.

in brief

The industry standard.

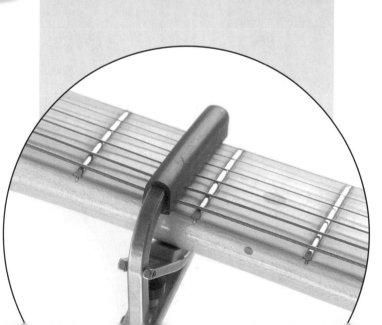

5. the Shubb 'deluxe' capo

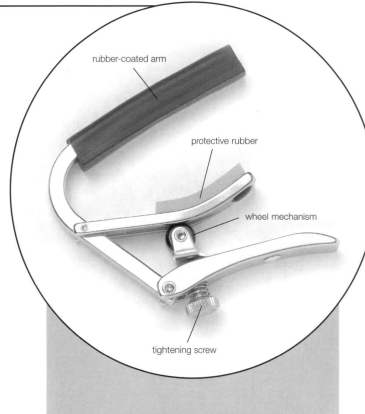

rubber-coated arm

protective rubber

wheel mechanism

tightening screw

Once Shubb had their design sorted out they had the good sense to develop a range of capos to suit different types of guitar with idiosyncratic necks. They make capos that will fit 12-string guitars, nylon 'classical' guitars, banjos, Dobros, and guitars with very curved fretboards.

The Deluxe, in a silver finish, resembles the Shubb 'Original' capo, but features an improved design. Instead of a simple screw/spring, the rubberized tip has been replaced by a tiny wheel which rolls back and forth on a groove imprinted into the underside of the middle 'jaw'.

This improved mechanism makes the lock and release action even smoother.

capo tips

The rubber 'finger' that holds down the strings has a slim profile. This means that when playing first fret chords right next to the capo your hand is less likely to bump into it.

in brief

A brilliant bit of kit.

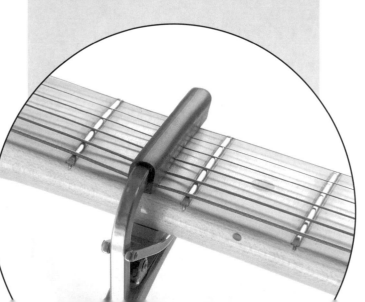

6. the Jim Dunlop picker's pal capo

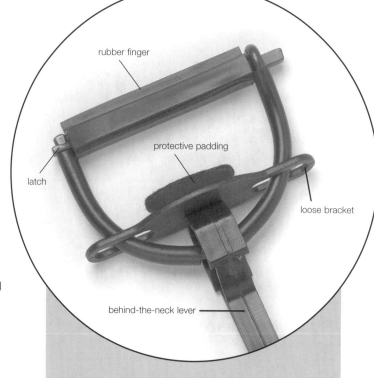

rubber finger

protective padding

latch

loose bracket

behind-the-neck lever

This capo is described as a 'universal capo' that will fit any guitar. It combines the 90 degree swivel of the old 'G' clamp idea with a variation of the behind-the-neck lock action of the Shubb design.

Laid out flat, this black capo looks like a 'Y' with an extra loose bracket fixed across it and the rubber finger opening at a right angle off the top of one of the Y's forks. The guitar neck is put in the open Y and the finger swivels across and hooks under a latch on the opposite top of the Y.

The behind-the-neck lever clamps horizontally toward the headstock (as opposed to the vertical Shubb method).

capo tips

This capo takes a little longer to get in place than the 'Clamp' models and you need to double-check that the strings are not buzzing.

in brief

Ideal for the guitar enthusiast with many different types of guitar.

7. the Kyser quick-change capo

This 'quick-change' capo is intended to fit any acoustic or electric guitar with curved frets. The company promise that it will not interfere with your playing and requires no adjustments. It's essentially a grip with two handles and a powerful spring. Squeeze the handles and the back pad and the rubber fingers open to allow you to slide the guitar neck inside. Then you just release the handles and the capo 'bites' the neck.

If it is positioned carefully this capo gives excellent first fret clearance. You can hold down a C chord and your first finger won't nudge the capo.

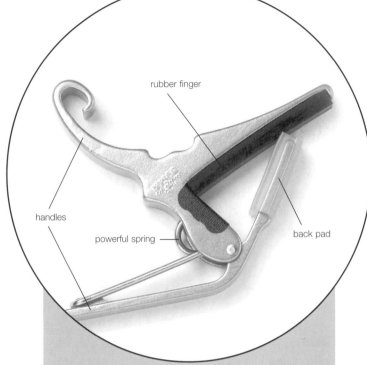

rubber finger

handles

powerful spring

back pad

capo tips

The beauty of this design is that the two handles point up. This means you can change capo position with your fretting hand only.

also available

Kyser make a range of capos, including the *Renaissance*, and a capo that imitates a 'drop D' tuning by only clamping the top five strings. Jim Dunlop's 'Trigger' capo has a similar design, while a distinctive variation is the 'Bird Of Paradise', with its bright orange 'beak' and plastic 'eye' hinge cover that appears to be looking at you.

in brief

A fine alternative to the Shubb design. Perfect for mid-song modulations.

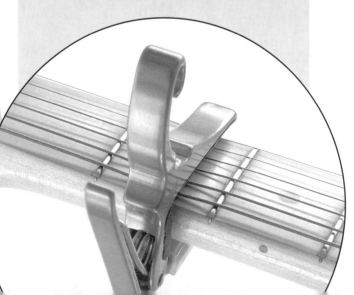

8. the glider capo

In this design, the rubber 'finger' is replaced with a rubber cylinder through which runs a rounded metal bar. Attached at either end is a spring. One end of the bar unscrews to allow the capo to be fitted to the guitar neck.

Behind the neck another metal rod is fitted with a molded rubber piece in an hour-glass shape. The tension of the springs holds the capo in position.

The extra feature, which gives the capo its name, is that it will roll from one fret to another if the fretting hand pushes the back-bar along the neck.

This means that it's possible to change capo positions in the middle of a song with only a fractional break in continuity.

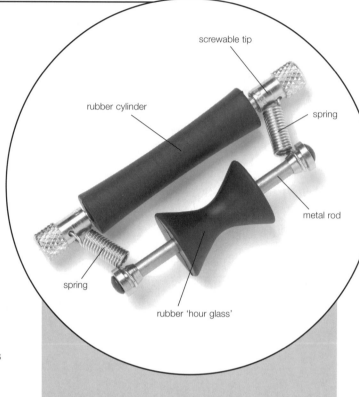

screwable tip
rubber cylinder
spring
metal rod
spring
rubber 'hour glass'

capo tips

The Glider can be left behind the nut when not is use.

in brief

One of the more expensive capos, but clever.

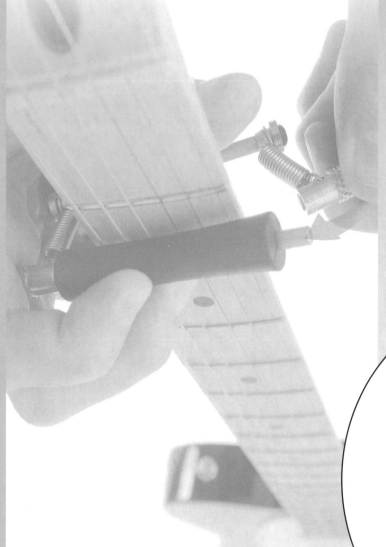

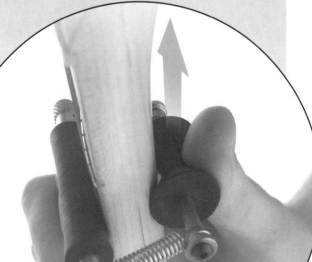

9. the Shubb partial capo

The partial capo allows adventurous guitarists to simulate open tunings without the hassle of actually retuning, providing easy access to unique sounds that standard tuning can't provide. It also removes the need for experimentally-minded players to try to 'adapt' standard capos, by cutting notches in them to stop the capo holding down all the strings.

The Shubb partial capo is designed to skip the outside strings (either bass or treble) and hold down three of the four inside strings. The design is a standard Shubb locking action but with a cut-down 'rubber finger' (the bit that holds down the strings) and a more curved metal arm, designed to clear the top or bottom strings with ease.

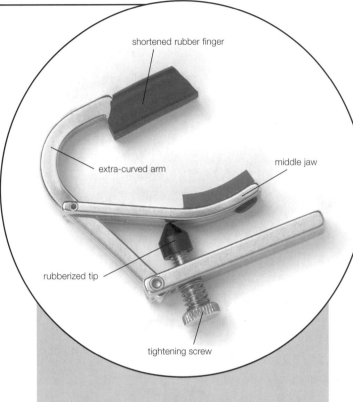

shortened rubber finger

extra-curved arm

middle jaw

rubberized tip

tightening screw

capo tips

Can take longer to fix in position but anyone experienced enough to want to mess around with one will be able to cope with any tuning adjustments.

in brief

If you love altered tunings, you'll love this.

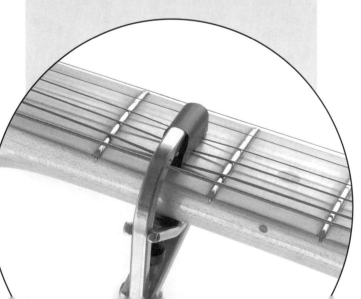

10. the third hand capo

This capo represents a further step of sophistication from the partial capo as it allows any combination of strings to be clamped at a given fret.

The design is similar to an elasticated capo but instead of the metal bar having a single plastic sheath it has six individual rubber 'washers'. These washers are mostly round but have one side that is flat, and can be rotated around the central metal bar. When the flat side is facing downwards it comes into contact with the string and clamps it; when it is facing upwards the string is left to vibrate freely.

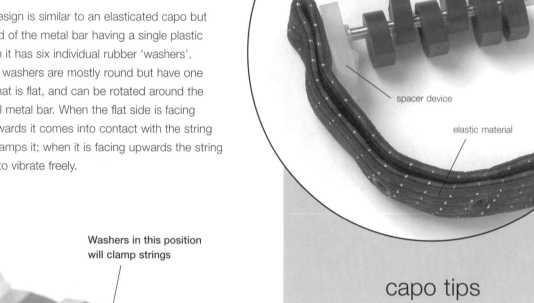

rubber washer

metal bar

spacer device

elastic material

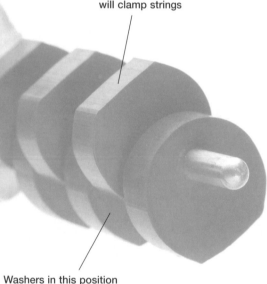

Washers in this position will clamp strings

Washers in this position allow strings to ring

The six washers can also be moved horizontally along the bar to match the spacing of the strings of your guitar and to take account of the widening of the neck at higher fret positions.

The small white plastic 'spacer' device sits on the edge of the fretboard and then the (very strong) elastic material is stretched round the back of the neck and hooks over the end of the metal bar to fix the capo in place.

capo tips

The capo seems to like some combinations more than others (I found some instability when attempting to get it to hold down the bass strings). Although this is a ground-breaking invention for the guitarist, I'm sure we haven't yet had the best version of the design.

In brief

A fascinating design which opens up all sorts of exciting musical possibilities. More details can be had at www.thirdhandcapo.com.

Each rubber washer rotates around the central metal bar to allow any combination of strings to be capoed

The Third Hand Capo comes with an exemplary sheet of information that not only describes some of its possibilities but also includes notation examples and chord boxes.

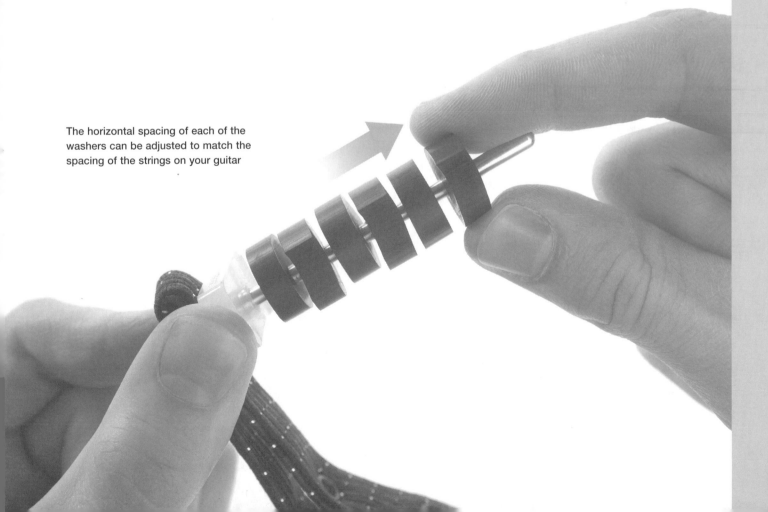

The horizontal spacing of each of the washers can be adjusted to match the spacing of the strings on your guitar

fitting your capo – dos and don'ts

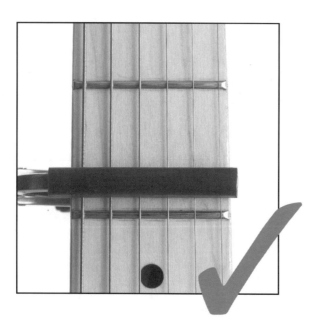

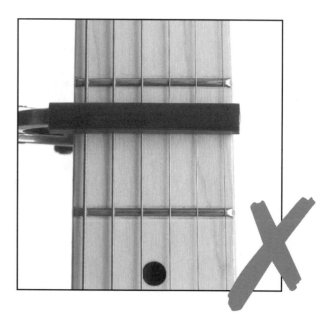

DO place the capo as close as you can to the fret above it. This will give you the cleanest sound and the best intonation.

However, it can also be problematic if you place the capo *too* close to the fret above. It can interfere with the movement of the fretting hand and the playing of chords and notes on the first fret past the capo.

DO pay attention to vertical positioning.

Make sure that your capo isn't pulling the strings up or down from their usual position.

DO use the right capo for the job.

A straight capo on a curved neck makes good contact on the inner strings but not on the outer top and bottom. Squeezing the capo at the bottom to cure that string problem usually leads to a problem with the top string and *vice versa*.

potential drawbacks of the capo

Great invention though it is, the capo has a number of operational problems. It is a good idea to be aware of these even though the best modern designs have eliminated or minimized them. First, some older models were quite heavy and unbalanced the guitar. Second, fitting a capo often affects the tuning of the guitar. This is because in order for the capo to allow the strings to ring clearly, and not to muffle them, it must exert a certain amount of pressure.

Capo exerts pressure on neck

Strings may be pulled out of position

This can effect the tension of the strings

Unfortunately, this pressure can cause the strings to go slightly sharp. The wire-wound bass strings are more vulnerable to this because they are thicker, and the heavier the gauge of strings the more noticeable the detuning effect.

This question of re-tuning doesn't matter so much in the recording studio. But it can be an issue in live performance if it causes a delay as the guitarist pauses to re-tune not only his own instrument but to double-check he is in tune with the other musicians.

The capo can also cause problems for the rock guitarist when bending strings. With a capo on the fourth fret a song in E major can be played with open chord shapes drawn from C major. This is great news for rhythm guitarists, but if the lead guitarist wants to take a solo he or she will find that the usual open strings and the first position E scales are unavailable. Secondly, strings that are bent on a capoed guitar often don't return to their original position, due to the clamping effect of the capo. This can be off-set if bending technique is adapted so the bending finger pulls the string back into position – but it isn't the same as having the freedom to bend at will!

capo basics

As I mentioned in the introduction, the capo is a wonderfully versatile bit of guitar gear, and there are numerous musical effects that you can create with one. However, before we explore some of the exciting possibilities that a capo opens up, let's get to grips with the basics.

At its simplest level, the capo allows you to take a chord sequence and move it any other key, without learning a whole set of new chord shapes.

Let's take a very simple example to demonstrate how this works. Try playing through this chord sequence using the simple open shapes given below:
Listen to **Track 3** to hear what this should sound like.

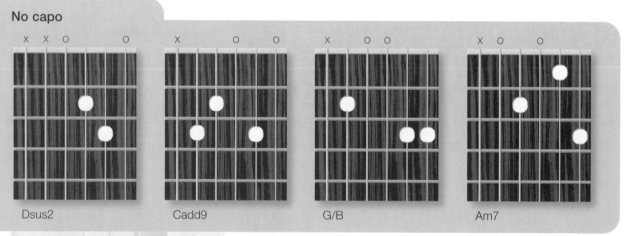

No capo

Dsus2   Cadd9   G/B   Am7

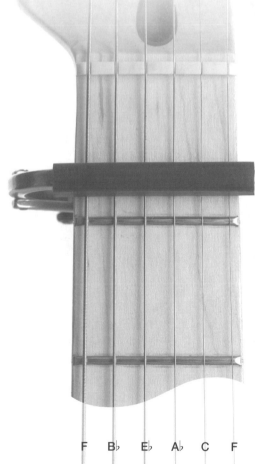

Now take your capo and attach it behind the first fret of your guitar.

The capo has now taken the place of the nut of your guitar, clamping all the strings at the first fret. Strum across the open strings and check that all six strings are ringing clearly. You should now be hearing the notes (from low to high) F B♭ E♭ A♭ C F. Check against **Track 4** to make sure.

You have effectively transposed your guitar up a semitone.

F   B♭   E♭   A♭   C   F

Now try playing through the same chord shapes as above. Although you're playing exactly the same shapes you will now create a set of chords which are all a semitone *above* the original set. Listen to **Track 5** to hear the effect and then compare back with **Track 3**, which is a semitone lower.

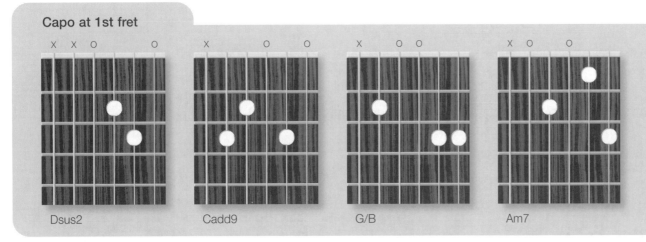

Capo at 1st fret

Dsus2   Cadd9   G/B   Am7

5

I'm willing to bet that you'll find playing this sequence with a capo easier than playing the equivalent chord shapes on an uncapoed guitar:

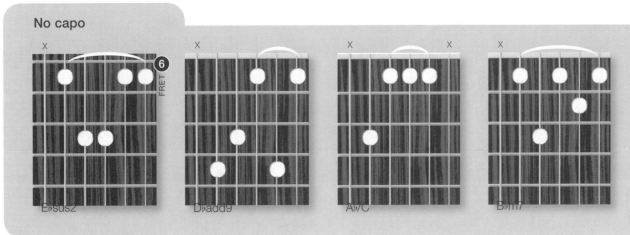

No capo

E♭sus2   D♭add9   A♭/C   B♭m7

Let's move the capo up another fret and play exactly the same set of shapes:

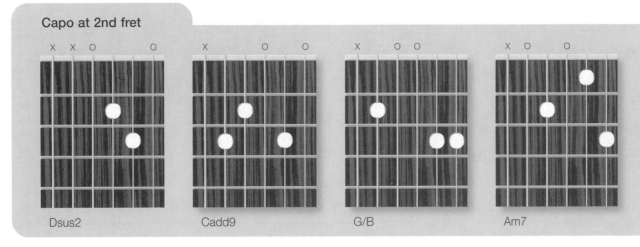

Capo at 2nd fret

Dsus2   Cadd9   G/B   Am7

6

As you can hear from **Track 6** the whole sequence is now a tone (two semitones) higher than when we started out.

Now try moving the capo up to the *fifth* fret. This will have the effect of moving the sequence up 5 semitones, or what classical musicians call a *perfect fourth*. So the same open shapes will now give the following sequence, which you can hear on **Track 7**:

The actual sounding chords are now Gsus2, Fadd9, C/E and Dm7, even though you're still playing the same familiar open shapes.

Capo at 5th fret

Dsus2

Cadd9

G/B

Am7

You will have noticed that as you move these shapes up the fretboard your hand position will get more and more cramped as the frets get closer together.

Open D shape

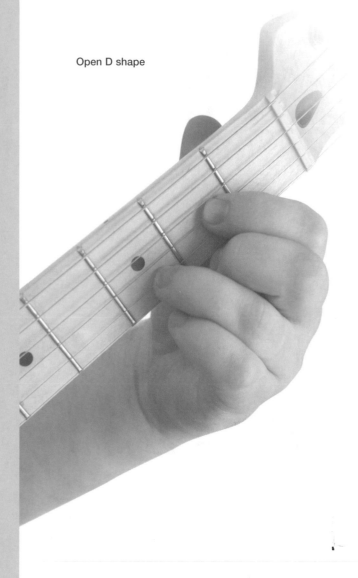

D shape at the 9th fret

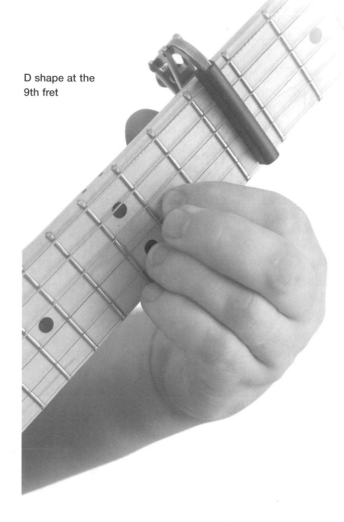

For many players this cramping is the limiting factor in how far up the neck they can play. Experiment and see how comfortable you are in these higher positions – it's different for everyone and depends on the size of your hands, how nimble and flexible you are, and the width of your guitar neck.

As an exercise, try this sequence of open chords in A major:

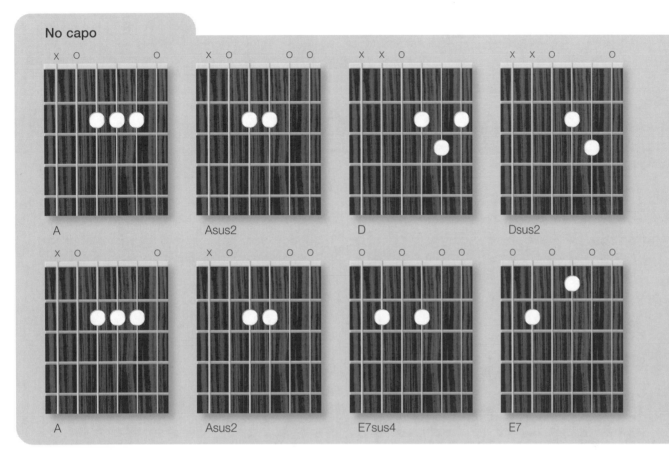

No capo

A   Asus2   D   Dsus2

A   Asus2   E7sus4   E7

You can hear this sequence demonstrated on **Track 8.**

Test yourself 1

Now try and figure out where you would have to put the capo to transpose this sequence into the following keys:

1. B major – **Track 9**

2. C♯ major – **Track 10**

3. D major – **Track 11**

4. E major – **Track 12**

Now let's see how this ability to transpose quickly while maintaining the same chord shapes can be put to use in a variety of musical situations.

4. 7th fret

3. 5th fret

2. 4th fret

1. 2nd fret

Answers:

transposing songs for singers

A capo is the easiest way of changing the key of a song so that it suits the range of your voice, or the voice of another singer. Of course, this was the reason that the capo was invented in the first place and it's still being used to solve the same problem today.

Imagine that you're a songwriter working on a song for your band. You've come up with a great chord progression and a beautiful melody, and you take it along to the next band rehearsal. But as you teach the song to the other members of the band it becomes clear that the singer's range simply won't allow them to sing the melody as you've written it.

There's no need to panic – simply strap on your capo and you can instantly transpose the song to any key you like, and still use the same chord shapes.

Imagine a song in G major, with the progression G - C - D - Em, like **Track 13:**

No capo

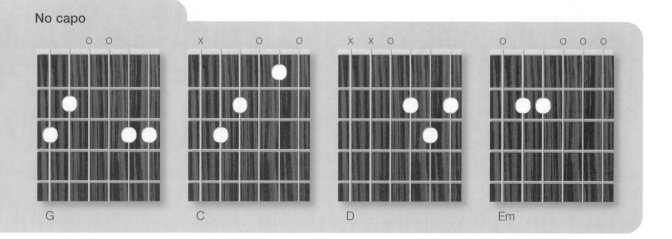

The chords are simple but let's say for the sake of argument the key is too low for your singer.

By fixing the capo at the third fret you can play the same open-string shapes to create the sounding chords of B♭, E♭, F and Gm:

Capo at 3rd fret

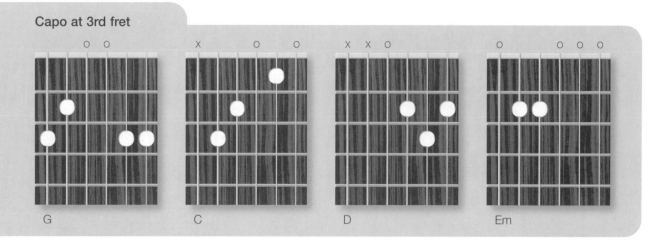

Not only are these chords easier to play than their barre versions, but the sound that you create will benefit from the ringing open strings, as you can hear on **Track 14**.

A capo can also bring a key *down* if the top notes of the melody are too high.

Imagine a classic descending sequence like the one on **Track 15:**

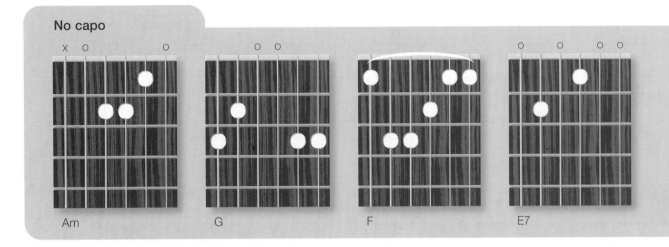

No capo

Am   G   F   E7

This could be brought down a tone by capoing at the 3rd fret and playing these shapes, as heard on **Track 16:**

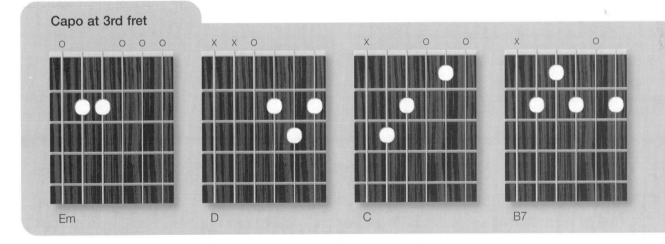

Capo at 3rd fret

Em   D   C   B7

The descending sequence now gives the sounding chords of Gm, F, E♭ and D7. It could be brought down another tone by simply playing the same shapes with a capo at the 1st fret.

the capo as a 'barre-reducer'

For the lazy guitarist (and let's face, most of us are) a capo allows you to avoid playing too many of those tricky barre chords. Take a look at the next example – a chord sequence in the key of E♭ minor, not a comfortable key for guitarists.

You have the following options:

1. Bite the bullet and just play the barre shapes
Listen to **Track 17** to hear the distinctive sound of these barre shapes.

No capo

2. Detune the entire guitar by a semitone
Track 18 demonstrates the laid-back feel that this generates.

Detuned by a semitone

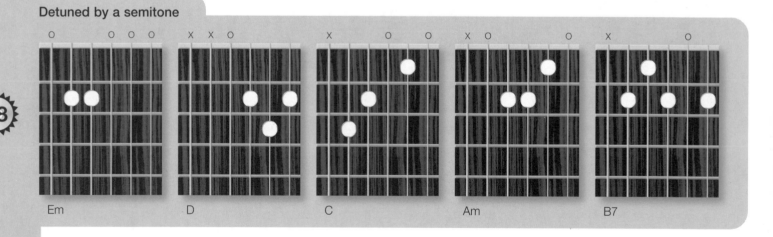

This is all well and good if you have a spare guitar permanently detuned by a semitone, or if you have a guitar tech on hand to take care of all your tuning needs.

For the rest of us, detuning and retuning can sometimes just be too much hassle.

3. Capo at Fret 1

Placing a capo at the first fret and playing these shapes will produce a very pleasing sound, as you can hear on **Track 19**:

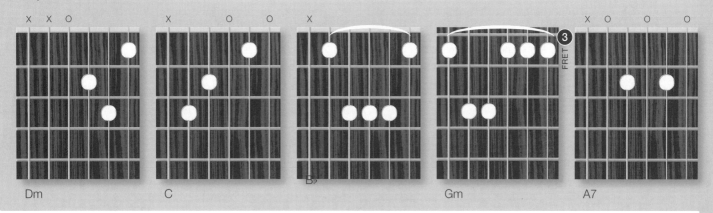

Dm   C   B♭   Gm   A7

4. Capo at Fret 6

Capoing at the 6th fret and playing these shapes produces a different, but no less pleasing, effect.

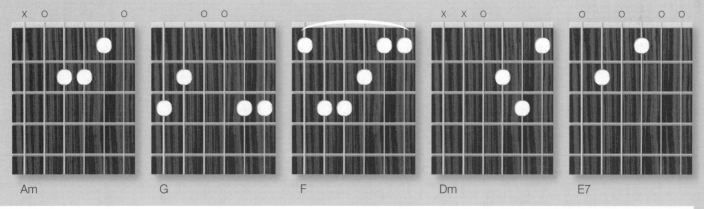

Am   G   F   Dm   E7

5. Capo at Fret 11

Finally, you could try a capo at the eleventh fret, and play these shapes to create a mandolin effect.

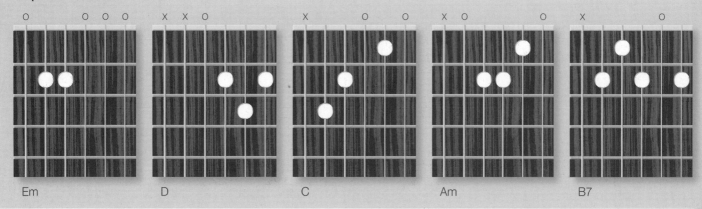

Em   D   C   Am   B7

To really understand this 'barre-reducing' principle, we need to look at the principle behind the *guitar-friendly* key.

guitar-friendly keys

The main use of the capo is to enable a player to work in keys which are unfavorable to the guitar without having to play endless barre chords. This is the stuff you really need to understand to get the most from your capo.

Most guitarists realize pretty quickly that there are some keys which are easier to play in than others or perhaps that there are some keys in which the guitar sounds better. With some instruments the question of which key you play in is not vital – for example, to a pianist there might be minor differences of fingering between playing in B♭ major and A major, but there isn't a substantial difference to the *sound quality*.

The guitar, however is moderately *key-sensitive*, meaning that sequences played in certain keys will sound appreciably different to the same sequence in other keys.

So what are the main factors that determine whether a key sounds good on the guitar?

1. Does the key scale (major or natural minor) contain notes that can be played as open strings?
Actually, the majority of keys will allow at least one open string, but it is more effective to have several. The more 'open string notes' a key has, the more likely you are to get open-string chord shapes that are resonant and easy to play. The six open strings (E, A, D, G, B and E) are all present in the keys of C, G, D (and their relative minors Am, Em and Bm).

C major

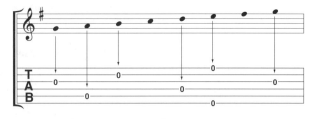

A natural minor

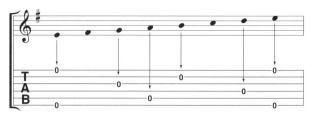

G major

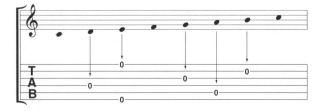

E natural minor

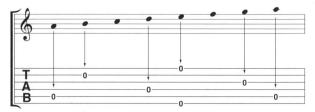

D major

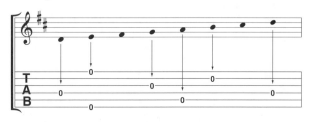

B natural minor

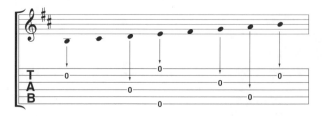

If we include mixolydian scales, with their lowered seventh, which are extensively used in all types of popular music, the key of A also begins to look very attractive:

A mixolydian

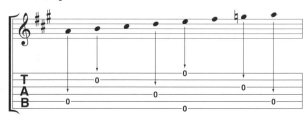

Notice that all the keys of G, D and A are all on the 'sharp side' of C major. C major requires no sharps or flats to make a major scale, G requires one sharp, D requires two and A requires three. The guitar has a natural bias toward the sharp keys and away from the flat keys. For example, as soon as we go into F major, the first flat key, we lose one of the open strings, B, which becomes B♭.

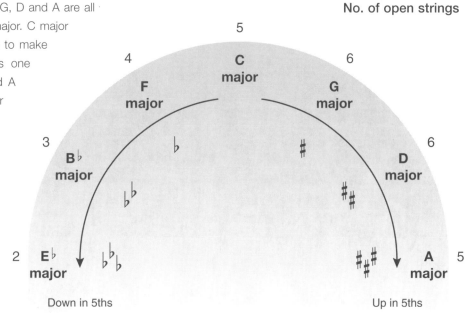

No. of open strings

Down in 5ths

Up in 5ths

2. Does the key allow a large number of open-string chord shapes?

The more open-string chords a key allows the easier it is to play in. Not only that, but open-string chords allow you to get more sound out of your instrument, especially on an acoustic guitar. This is because an unfretted string produces more volume than a fretted one.

Just listen to **Track 22** to hear the difference between open chord shapes and their barre equivalents:

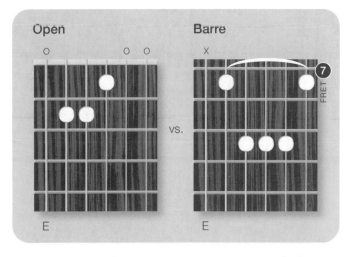

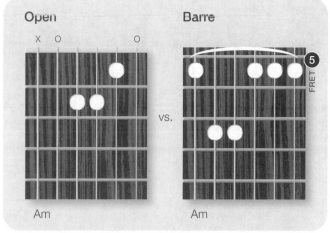

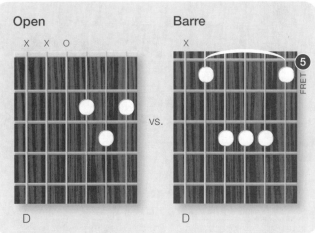

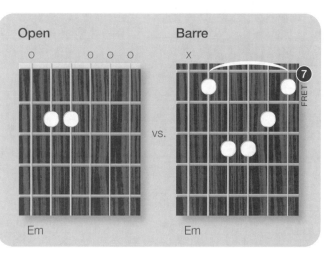

Let's look at one of our candidates for a guitar-friendly key, C major. C major's primary chords for songs are C Dm Em F G and Am, and B dim (which is rarely used).

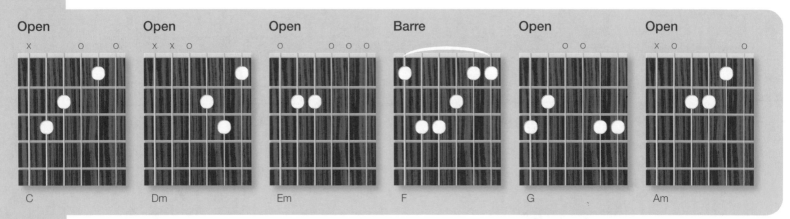

C	Dm	Em	F	G	Am

Among the six most commonly-used chords there is only one barre chord – F. We can easily remove that by replacing it with Fmaj7, which is why in guitar tutor books beginners are often taught to play Fmaj7 before F.

Now compare the chords of C with those of E major, which requires four barre chords:

Fmaj7

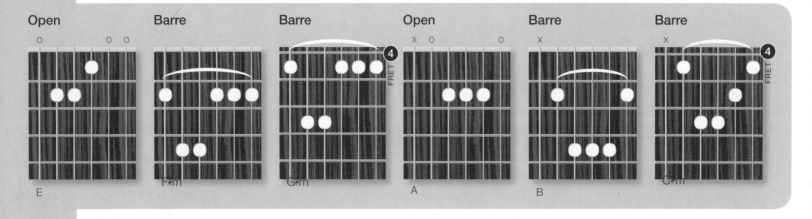

E	F#m	G#m	A	B	C#m

Or Bb major, which needs five:

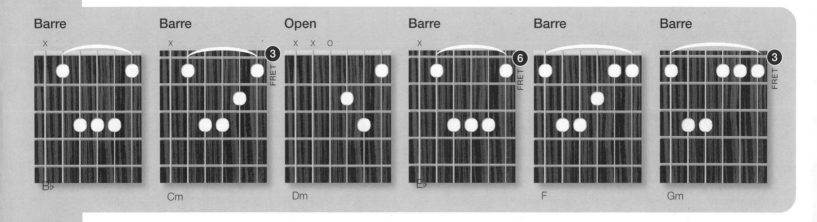

Bb	Cm	Dm	Eb	F	Gm

So, to summarise: the main guitar-friendly keys are F, C, G, D, A and E. A capo simply allows you to put a difficult flat or sharp key into the guise of one of these.

To work out your options with any chord progression simply consult the table opposite. It is built on the eight basic open chord shapes (at the head of the table).

How to use the table:

1. Establish the key of the piece of music (this will often be the first or last chord in the song, or can be determined from the key signature)

2. Locate the different places in the table where the key chord occurs

3. Choose the capo position that includes the largest number of the other chords in the song

Fret	A	C	D	E	G	Am	Dm	Em
I	A#/Bb	C#/Db	D#/Eb	F	G#/Ab	A#m/Bbm	D#m/Ebm	Fm
II	B	D	E	F#/Gb	A	Bm	Em	F#m/Gbm
III	C	D#/Eb	F	G	A#/Bb	Cm	Fm	Gm
IV	C#/Db	E	F#/Gb	G#/Ab	B	C#m/Dbm	F#m/Gbm	G#m/Abm
V	D	F	G	A	C	Dm	Gm	Am
VI	D#/Eb	F#/Gb	G#/Ab	A#/Bb	C#/Db	D#m/Ebm	G#m/Abm	A#m/Bbm
VII	E	G	A	B	D	Em	Am	Bm
VIII	F	G#/Ab	A#/Bb	C	D#/Eb	Fm	A#m/Bbm	Cm
IX	F#/Gb	A	B	C#/Db	E	F#m/Gbm	Bm	C#m/Dbm
X	G	A#/Bb	C	D	F	Gm	Cm	Dm

A couple of examples will make this clear:

Let's imagine you have some sheet music for a song written on the piano. The key is Ab major and almost every chord involves a barre.

You want to use the capo to find an easier way to play in the key of Ab major:

1. Look on the table for the first Ab chord. The first is in column 5, on the first line.

2. Look upward and you see that this Ab chord is in the 'G' column. Look left and you will see it is at the first fret. This means that if you put the capo at the first fret and play a G shape, the chord you will actually hear is Ab. Check through the song and see if you can find open-string equivalents for all the chords with the capo at the first fret.

So, capoing at fret 1 may well provide you with all the open shapes you need to play through the song. However, there are other possibilities:

Option 2
The next Ab on the table occurs on line 4, column 4, as an E shape, so you could capo at the fourth fret and play an E shape to create the key chord of Ab.

Option 3
The one after that falls in column 3 on the sixth line. So the Ab key chord could be played with as a D shape with a capo at the 6th fret.

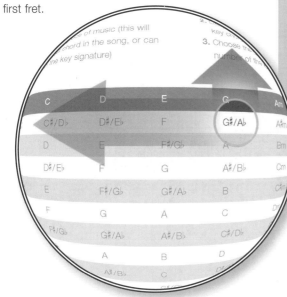

Test yourself 2

Try reading off the possible capo positions for the following chords:

1. Eb major (4 possibilities)

2. Eb minor (2 possibilities)

3. Bb major (5 possibilities)

Answers:

1. Capo 1st fret, D shape; capo 3rd fret, C shape; capo 6th fret, A shape; capo 8th fret, G shape.

2. Capo 1st fret, Dm shape; capo 6th fret, Am shape.

3. Capo 1st fret, A shape; capo 3rd fret, G shape; capo 6th fret, E shape; capo 8th fret, D shape; capo 10th fret, C shape.

Finally, try the following chord sequence in D♭ major:

No capo

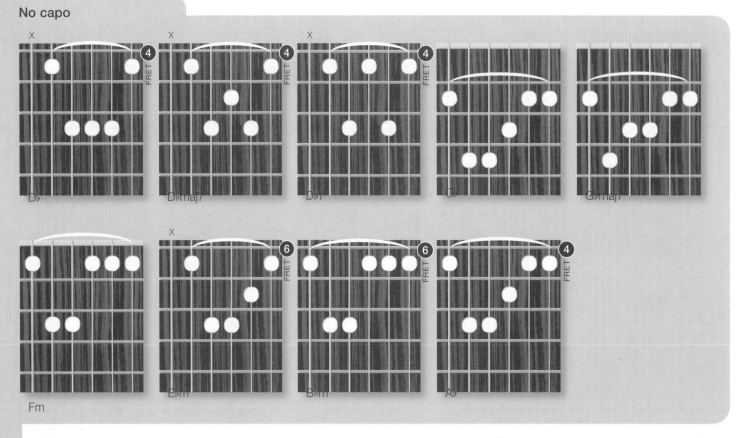

Fm   E♭m   B♭m   A♭

Without a capo every chord is a barre!

But put a capo at the first fret and play as if in C major and it turns into:

Capo 1st fret

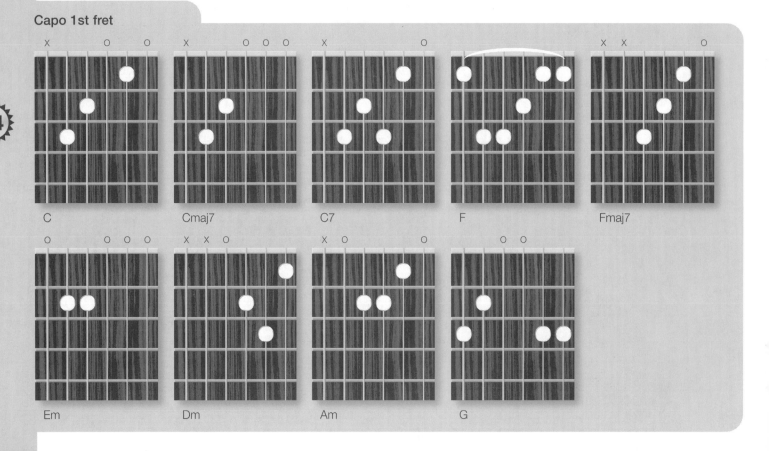

C   Cmaj7   C7   F   Fmaj7

Em   Dm   Am   G

Now the only barre that's required is for the F and the whole sequence is much easier to play and sounds better too!

tone and feel

An interesting side-effect of the capo is that it changes the feel, playability and tone of the guitar. Once again, this contributes to the overall sound, and gives effects that can't be obtained in any other way.

For example, if the string tension on your guitar feels too tight, try tuning a semi-tone below concert pitch and put a capo at the first fret, or even tune a tone down with the capo at the second fret.

Listen to **Track 25**, which features guitars in standard tuning, and compare the quality of the sound with **Track 26**, which features guitars tuned down by a tone and then capoed at the 2nd fret.

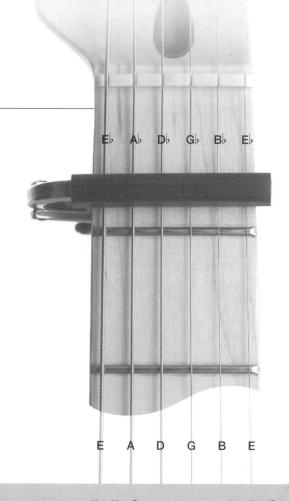

Capo at 2nd fret

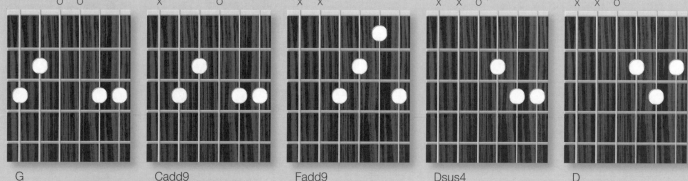

| G | Cadd9 | Fadd9 | Dsus4 | D |

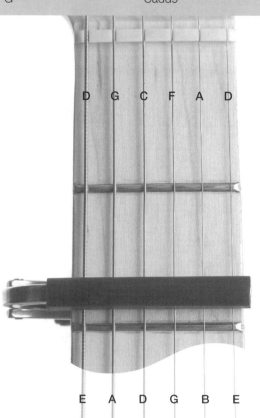

This trick is often used with 12-string guitars to reduce the considerable tension on the neck, and therefore make it easier for the left hand to fret chords (already more difficult than on a 6-string because of the additional sets of strings).

It has the additional benefit of reducing the number of high G strings (an octave above the standard third string) that you are likely to snap.

As you move your capo further up the neck, the sound quality of the guitar changes even more noticeably.

With the loss of low bass notes and the addition of more high notes, the guitar takes a step toward the mandolin's territory as you can hear on **Track 27**:

Capo at 7th fret

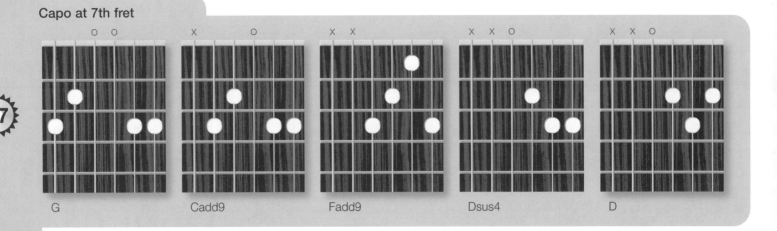

G   Cadd9   Fadd9   Dsus4   D

An added benefit of capoing this high up is that you get to play chord shapes further up the neck where the frets are closer together and the neck is wider. (Anyone who has ever tried playing an open C shape on a Rickenbacker 12-string will understand about the problems of narrow necks.)

You may well find that some shapes that you simply can't manage down at the first fret become much more approachable further up the neck.

As you will discover with a little experimentation, a whole new world of chord shapes opens up once you have the ability to stretch further than three or four frets.

Try the shapes on the right with your capo at the 7th fret. If you have problems stretching any of these shapes, just move the capo up another couple of frets and try again!

Capo at 7th fret

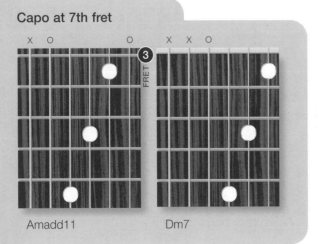

Amadd11   Dm7

Many of these shapes are suited to finger-picking, especially these two, as you can hear on **Track 28**.

Capo at 7th fret

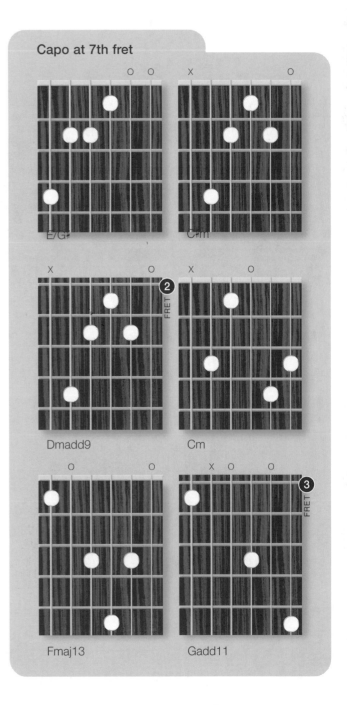

E/G#   C#m

Dmadd9   Cm

Fmaj13   Gadd11

40

know where the notes are

This is possibly the most useful and fascinating fact about working with a capo:

> No matter where you capo your guitar if you fret a note above the capo it will give you the same pitch as if the guitar was uncapoed.

This is great news if you need to switch between rhythm playing, where you want to play some beautiful full-sounding open chords, and lead playing, where it's vital that you can use fretboard shapes and licks that are familiar to you from playing an uncapoed guitar.

Track 29 demonstrates a classic 12-bar sequence in E major, using A7, D7 and E7 shapes, played by the rhythm guitar with a capo at the 7th fret.

Play through the track once using these chord shapes and then try taking a solo over the backing using familiar E pentatonic shapes at the 12th fret.

All your familiar reference points on the fretboard still hold true, which helps immensely when soloing. Not only that, but any barre or moveable chord shapes that you know will still work on a capoed guitar.

Capo at 7th fret

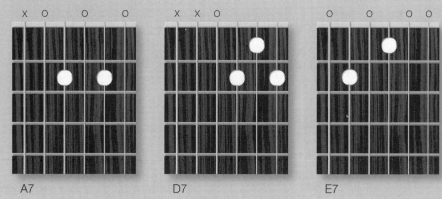

A7   D7   E7

Imagine that you're working on a song with the chord progression F♯m – A – Bsus2 – C♯. Playing this sequence on an uncapoed guitar involves playing three barre chords (F♯m, Bsus2 and C♯). Listen to **Track 30** to hear what this sounds like.

But put a capo at the 2nd fret and it can be played like this:

Capo at 2nd fret

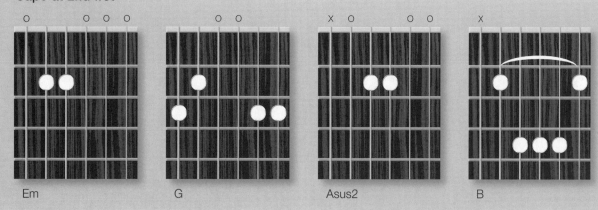

Em   G   Asus2   B

Note that the fourth shape is exactly the same in both examples – an A barre shape at the 4th fret.

Because the shape doesn't contain any open strings it's not affected by the capo.

working with two guitars

If you are working with another guitarist, or multi-tracking guitar parts, a capo can be used to double a chord sequence in different positions. This gives a fuller texture and can approximate a 12-string even if you don't have one.

For example, an extreme, but simple 'doubling' effect can be achieved like this:

Guitar 1 plays a set of simple open chord shapes. Guitar 2 plays the same set of shapes, but with a capo at the 12th fret, thus creating the same chords an octave higher.

Try it for yourself with this chord sequence, which you can hear on **Track 32**.

Now listen to the doubled version, on **Track 33**. The feasibility of this technique will depend on the following factors:
• What type of guitar is used
• How good is its intonation is above the 12th fret
• What the key is, which will determine whether you can get your fingers between the frets.

If an acoustic proves impossible for the task, a clean-toned electric guitar on its bridge pickup will be an acceptable substitute in a multi-track recording.

Capo at 12th fret

32
Guitar 1 only

33
Guitars 1 & 2

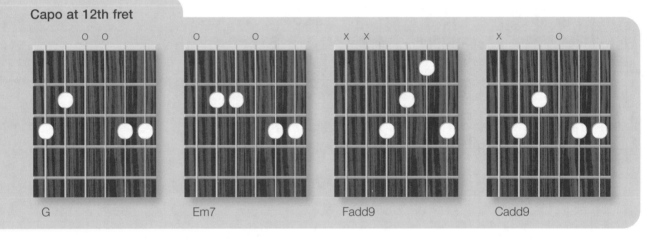

G   Em7   Fadd9   Cadd9

A more common technique is to create two guitar parts which follow the same sequence, but which use the capo to allow contrasting chord shapes (and therefore voicings) to be used. For example, if Guitar 1 plays a sequence in C major using open chords, and Guitar 2 plays the same

sequence with a capo at the 5th fret, using different shapes, the overall sound will be tonally rich.

Try this example, and then listen to **Track 34** to hear the basic (no capo) chords, and **Track 35** to hear the full effect:

Guitar 1: no capo

34
Guitar 1 only

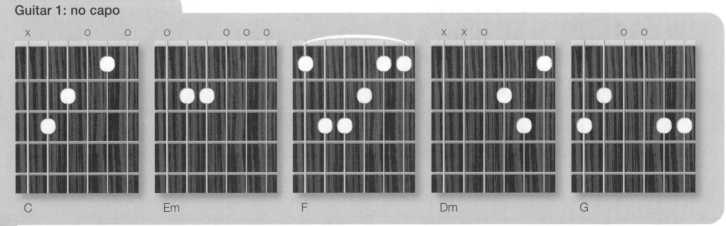

C   Em   F   Dm   G

Guitar 2: capo at 5th fret

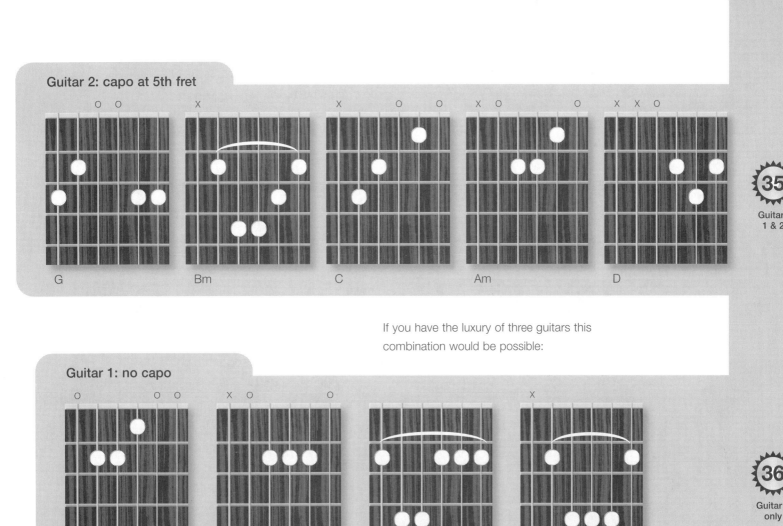

G   Bm   C   Am   D

35

Guitars
1 & 2

If you have the luxury of three guitars this combination would be possible:

Guitar 1: no capo

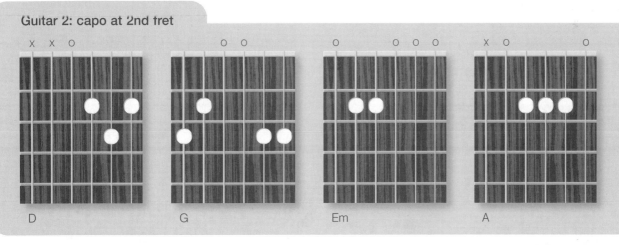

E   A   F#m   B

36

Guitar 1
only

Guitar 2: capo at 2nd fret

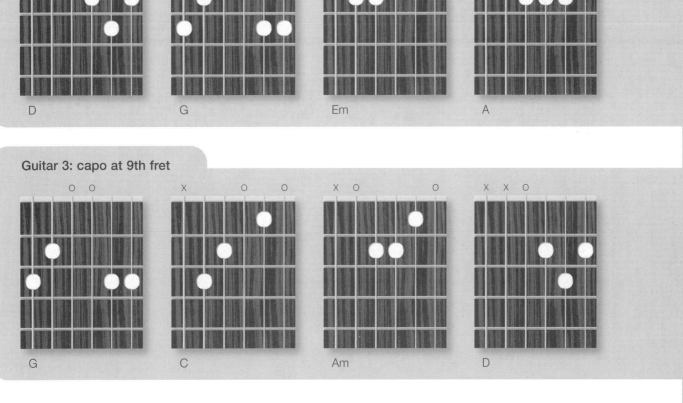

D   G   Em   A

37

Guitars
1 & 2

Guitar 3: capo at 9th fret

G   C   Am   D

38

Guitars
1, 2 & 3

In the next example, let's assume that we have a chord sequence in the key of G major and we want to find out what the options are for a second capoed guitar. Here's the basic chord sequence:

Guitar 1: no capo

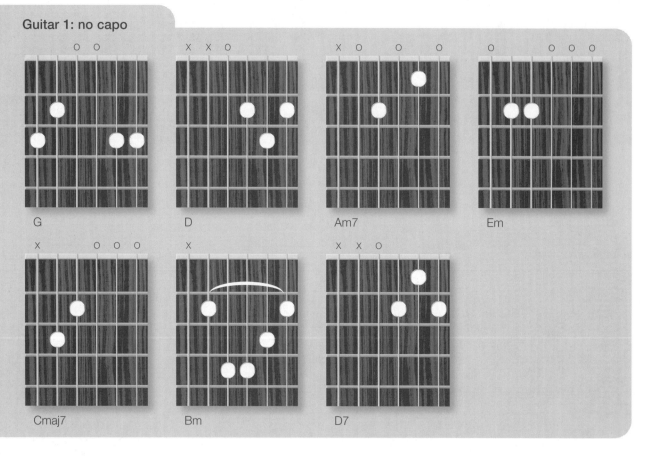

You need look for a capo position where you can maximize the number of open-string chords, and you'll probably favor capo positions higher up the neck to provide the strongest possible contrast with Guitar 1. (Although of course, the higher up the neck the capo is clamped the trickier it might be to hold some of the shapes.) Here are the four possible options; in each case listen to the audio examples to hear the effect:

Option 1 - Guitar 2: capo at 3rd fret

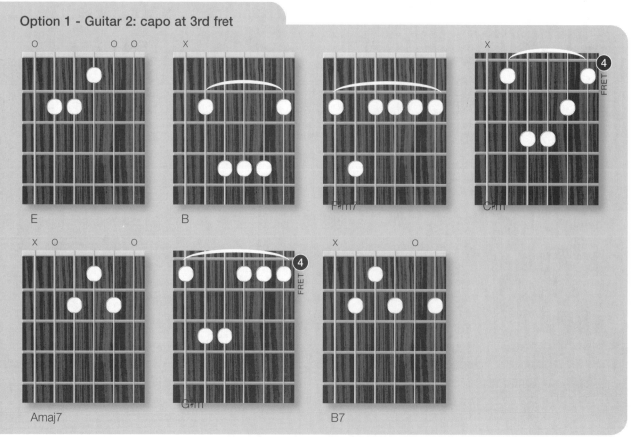

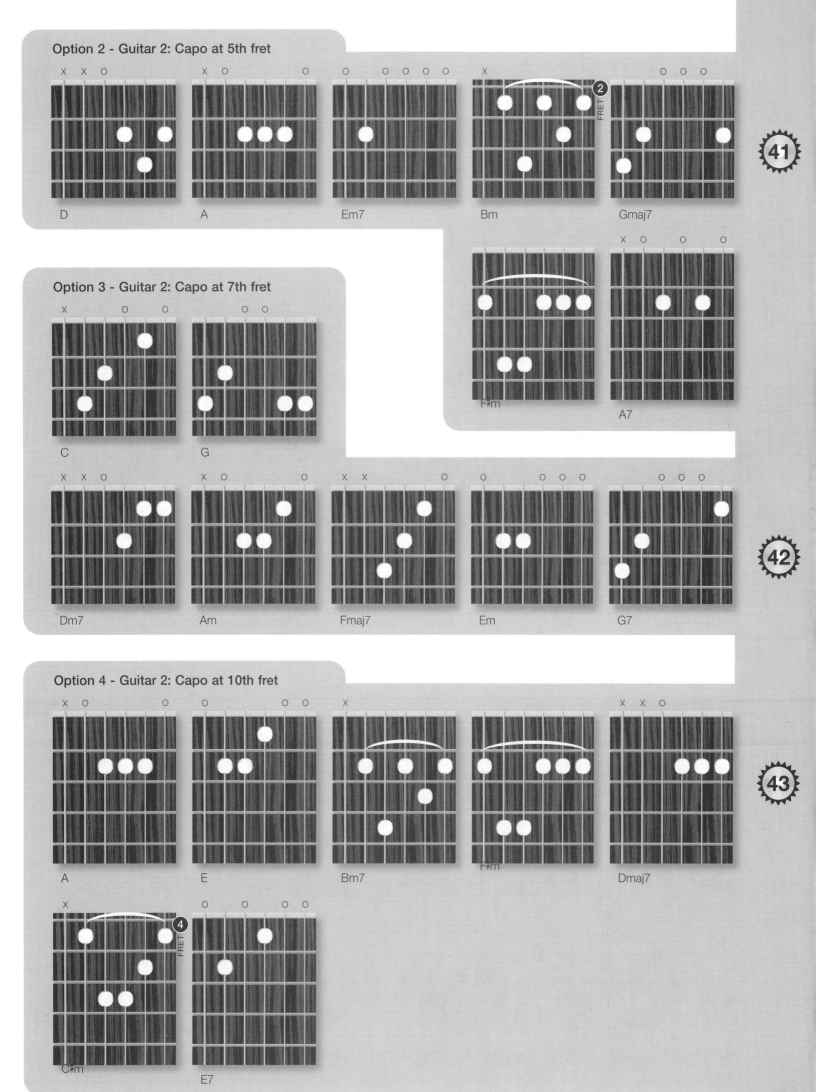

capo tricks for arrangers

Sometimes a capo can be really handy when you're trying to arrange a song for solo guitar with vocal, or create an instrumental version. The most frequently encountered challenge is when a chord sequence has a descending bass-line. Imagine that you're trying to create a guitar part to represent the following chord sequence (where the descending bass-line would originally have been played by a bass guitar):

No capo

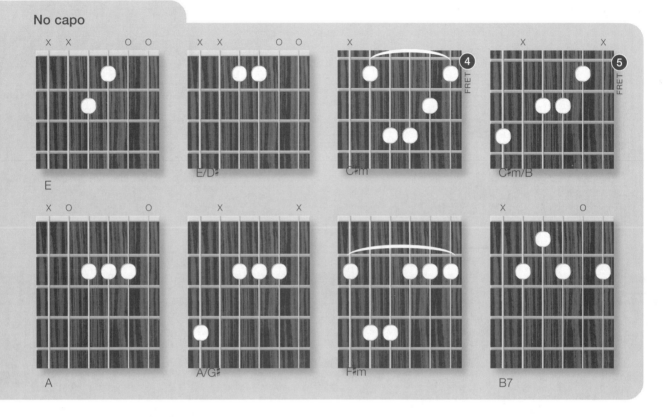

It's very difficult to get a smooth effect it you play this sequence on an uncapoed guitar. The trick is to use a capo to transpose the chord shapes into the keys of D, C and G, which will each allow a descending bass-line to be played under the relevant chords:

Capo at 2nd fret

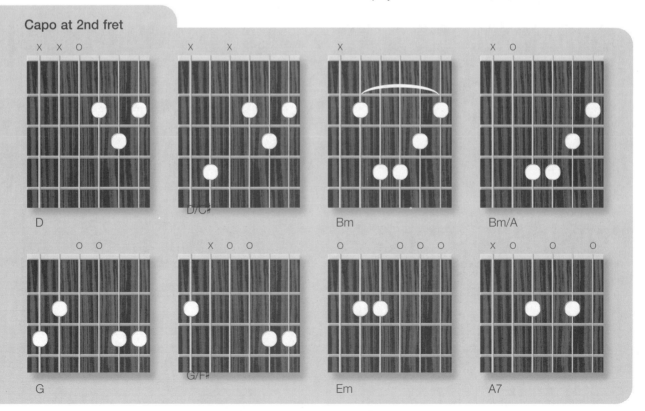

A similar arranging problem can sometimes occur when transcribing a song originally written for piano, which is likely to contain plenty of inversions. For a start, a song conceived on the piano is unlikely to be in a 'guitar-friendly' key such as E or A. In this example a relatively simple chord progression is made challenging for guitarists because of the key of A♭ and the many inversions.

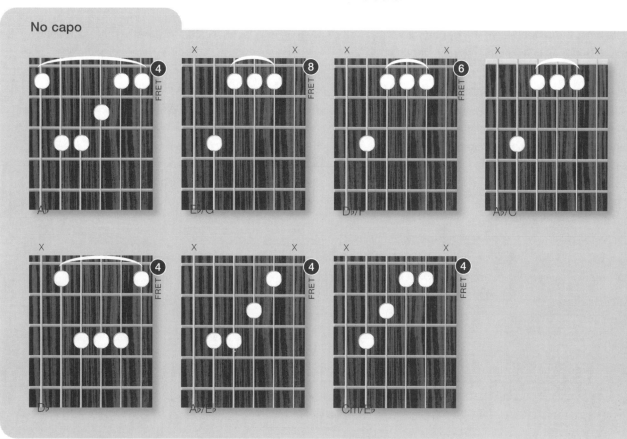

No capo

However, armed with your trusty capo, you can simply transpose the chord shapes into a key where there are some easy inversion shapes:

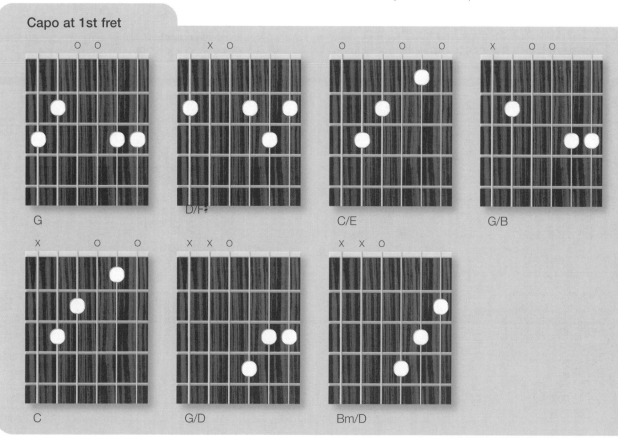

Capo at 1st fret

capos and doubleneck guitars

While most of us don't have the opportunity to explore the possibilities of combining capos and doubleneck guitars, if you do get a chance then it can be a most rewarding exercise. Although doubleneck guitars tend to be thought of as eye-catching gimmicks brandished by heavy rock guitar heroes, they can offer some interesting musical avenues to explore in which the capo can play a role.

With the standard doubleneck configuration of 12 string/ 6 string the player has the chance to not only combine these two sounds in a single song, but also perhaps to combine two different tunings and to further extend this by using a capo on one or both necks.

Jimmy Page is, of course, the guitarist most associated with the red Gibson electric doubleneck, and a fine example of the interesting effects that can be obtained from this instrument can be found on his album *No Quarter* (with Robert Plant, 1994). On the track 'Wonderful One' he plays an acoustic 12/6 guitar. The lower, six-string neck is tuned G♭ G♭ D♭ G♭ D♭ G♭ while the 12-string is capoed in standard tuning at the first fret. The verses are played on the six-string; the chorus is played on the capoed 12-string, providing a highly effective contrast.

capos and altered tunings

Altered tunings have become increasingly popular with guitarists, offering a variety of new tonal possibilities. Perhaps the simplest alteration from standard tuning is to maintain the intervallic relationships between the strings, while simply tuning the whole guitar down a semitone or tone. This technique has become hugely popular amongst 'nu-metal' guitarists, who relish the increased 'grunginess' that it creates.

Unfortunately this is one area in which your capo won't be of much use to you. However, it may help if you want to play in either of the popular open tunings of Open A (E A E A C♯ E) or open E (E B E G♯ B E), which involve tuning a number of strings *above* standard pitch, risking string breakage and increasing tension. Many players don't mind doing this on an electric but are more nervous when it comes to doing the same thing on an acoustic guitar, with its heavier strings.

Open A tuning ➤	E	A	E	A	C♯	E
Difference in pitch from standard tuning ➤ (in semitones)	0	0	+2	+2	+2	0

A capo can be used in this situation to raise the pitch of an open or altered tuning to the desired level and avoid the risk of string breakage. In this example, you could tune to open G and open D (the equivalents a tone down) and put a capo at the second fret

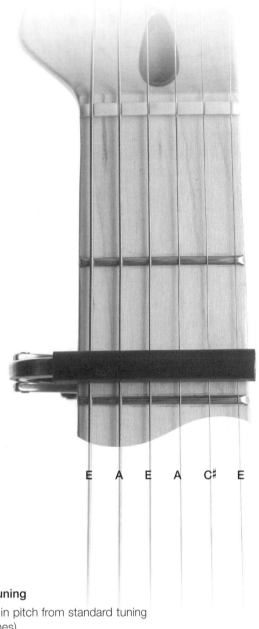

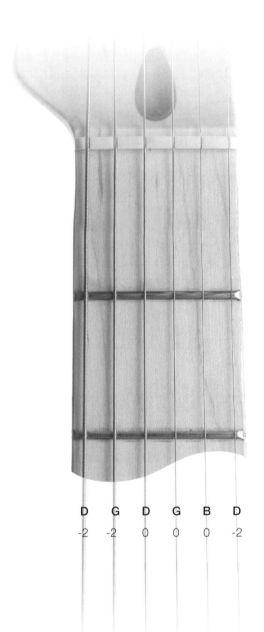

D	G	D	G	B	D	← **Open G tuning**
-2	-2	0	0	0	-2	← Difference in pitch from standard tuning (in semitones)

E A E A C♯ E

If you like open tunings and play live, a capo is one way to get several songs from the same tuning without playing several songs back to back in the same key, and without slowing proceedings by constant re-tuning. Just use the capo to change the tuning's pitch, as Keith Richards does with the Rolling Stones. Having developed a liking for open G tuning he tried it with a capo at the fourth fret, which gives open B tuning, and this led to songs like 'Tumbling Dice' and 'Happy'. (Of course, having lots of guitars and roadies to tune them and hand them to you also helps.) If you don't want to play in exactly the same open tuning a single string alteration, along with the capo change, will make all the difference.

As we've already seen capos can help with transposing for the sake of a singer, and this applies even more to altered tunings, since you're unlikely to be able to transpose your open tuning chord shapes 'on the fly'.

Imagine that you have a song in open D tuning (D A D F♯ A D), which was a good key for you to sing in, but not for the new vocalist who has just joined your band. They want to sing it in G, a fourth higher. You could move the song into open G tuning (D G D G B D), but you may well find that some of the best chord shapes are lost. The simplest solution is to stay in open D and capo at the 5th fret.

capo detection – use your ears!

If you ever try to work out songs by ear, being aware of the possibilities of capo usage can save you a lot of time. For example, if the song you're trying to figure out is played with a capo and you don't realize, you may end up playing some unnecessarily difficult chord shapes. Not only that, but you won't be able to capture the ringing sound of the original record.

With a little experience it is possible to educate your ear to recognize the tell-tale sounds of a capoed guitar. Here's a brief list of things to listen out for:

1. If you find that the song is in an unusually sharp or flat key (such as B♭ minor or D♭ major) which involves the use of a lot of barre chords then chances are you should be using a capo.

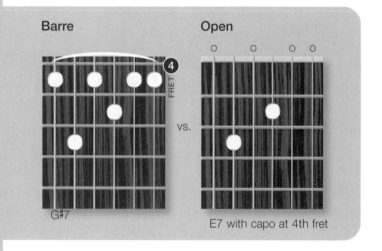

Barre

Open

G♯7

E7 with capo at 4th fret

2. Listen out for chords that sound particularly 'ringy', but which you would ordinarily have to play as a barre chord. Check out the two versions of G♯7 on **Track 48** to hear the difference.

3. Listen out for passages where the fretting hand is obviously playing embellishments that wouldn't be possible with a barre chord, as demonstrated on **Track 49.**

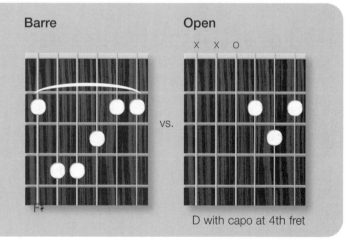

Barre

Open

F♯

D with capo at 4th fret

4. Does the song sound as though it was originally written on the piano? Pianists often use keys like E♭, D♭ or A♭ and the guitarist on the record may have capoed to get round this problem.

5. Listen for the distinctive higher-pitched, more trebly sound of a capoed guitar.

advanced capo-spotting

The real key to recognizing a capo from a recording is training your ear to hear the difference in chord voicing between the open shapes of **A, C, D, E, G, Am, Dm and Em**. These are the crucial shapes for the guitar and that's why they were at the head of the columns in the previous table.

Let's start with the shapes of A, C, D, E and G. Although these chords are all harmonically identical (they are all major triads) each chord shape produces a different *voicing* due to differences in the way the chords are structured. A particular voicing is characterized by:

1. The *number* of notes in each voicing

2. The *octave* in which those notes occur

3. The *order* in which the notes are stacked

4. The number and position of *open strings*

5. The note that appears at the *top* of the voicing

For example, this chord of E major could be characterized by this list:

1. It uses all six strings

2. The voicing spans two octaves

3. It includes 3 Es, 2 Bs and one G♯,

4. It uses 3 open strings

5. The top note is the root (E)

However, this chord of D major differs in every category:

1. It uses only four strings

2. It spans an octave and a third

3. It includes 2 Ds, one A and an F♯

4. It uses only one open string

5. The top note is the third (F♯)

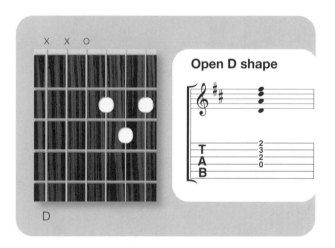

If you can train your ear to recognize these characteristics you'll be able to spot when a capo is being used.

Often the last of these characteristics is the most useful when trying to figure out which chord shape is being used. The five open major chord shapes can be divided up like this:

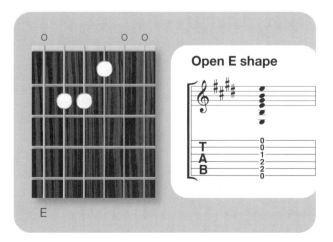

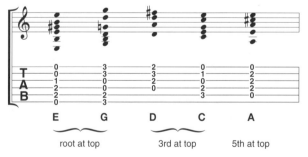

Test yourself 3

Try this test, paying special attention to the note at the top of each chord.

Listen to these four E chords and try and spot which chord shape is being used, and therefore, which fret the guitar is capoed at:

1. Track 50

2. Track 51

3. Track 52

4. Track 53

Test yourself 4

The three open minor shapes can also be distinguished by listening out for their top notes:
Root at top: E minor shape
Third at top: D minor shape
Fifth at top: A minor shape

Try the same exercise with these three E minor chords:

1. Track 54

2. Track 55

3. Track 56

special cases

The keys of E♭ major and A♭ major are special instances. If you're working out a song and you think that it may be in E♭ or A♭ then rather than a capo, the most likely explanation is that the whole guitar has been *tuned down*.

Tuning down means that each string is tuned down by the same amount. So for example the standard tuning of E A D G B E could be tuned down by a semitone to E♭ A♭ D♭ G♭ B♭ E♭, or by a tone to D G C F A D. This has four benefits:

1. It makes singing easier
2. It makes string-bending easier
3. It enables heavier gauge strings to be used more comfortably
4. It creates lower-pitched chords suitable for heavy rock

To check whether a song in E♭ is played on a detuned guitar listen out for the low bass E♭. If you can hear this note, which is below the range of a standard tuned guitar, the guitar must be de-tuned. If you can't hear the low E sounding and the E♭ chord sounds more like a D shape (i.e. with the third on top) the chances are there

is a capo at the 1st fret on a guitar in standard tuning. If the E♭ chord sounds like a C shape the capo is at the 3rd fret.

Another clue is that there is often a relationship between the instrumentation and style of a song and its key, and therefore the use of a capo. For example, brass instruments tend to use flat keys like E♭ and B♭. So if a record has brass instruments on it (like a 1960s soul song) it may well be in a flat key. The guitarists on the original session would probably have managed without a capo because they were only playing 'partial' chords, or decorative figures. They were only *part* of the harmony, not the whole harmony. If you play such songs with a band then you won't need to worry about a capo either. But if you want to do a busker's solo acoustic version then you will need to play full chords, hopefully with open strings ringing, and have fingers free for embellishments, so you'll want to use a capo.

Where flat keys occur in heavy rock and blues they generally indicate detuning rather than a capo, whereas a flat key in more introspective, folky, acoustic-type material is generally an indication that a capo has been used.

Answers 4:
1. Am shape   Capo 7th fret
2. Open Em   no capo
3. Dm shape   Capo 2nd fret

Answers 3:
1. D shape   Capo 2nd fret
2. A shape   Capo 7th fret
3. Open E   no capo
4. G shape   capo 9th fret

ADVANCED TECHNIQUES

the partial capo

Most guitarists find it relatively easy to get used to the conventional capo as it affects all six strings simultaneously. The **partial** capo is a more advanced tool that allows complex effects to be created due to the fact that it holds down some of the strings, leaving the others unaffected.

The simplest way of getting a partial capo effect is to use a regular capo across the top five or bottom five strings, leaving either the top or bottom string uncapoed. Most clamp-style capos will allow you to do this, although there are special capos specifically designed for this purpose.

Try capoing the top five strings at the second fret. This will give you the effect of a Drop D tuning without any retuning:

All the standard D shapes (now sounding in E) will benefit from the low E string ringing out:

Partial capo at 2nd fret (strings 1-5)

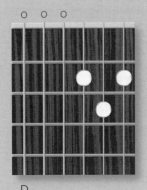

D

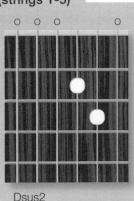

Dsus2

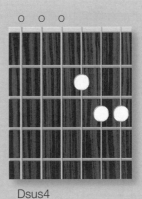

Dsus4

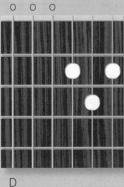

D

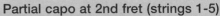

57

Now try reversing the capo so that the bottom five strings are capoed at the second fret:

Play some familiar open chord shapes and notice how the ringing top E string produces some interesting effects:

Partial capo at 2nd fret (strings 2-6)

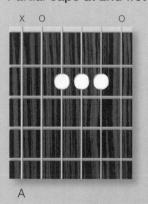
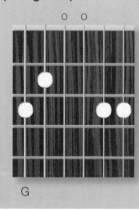
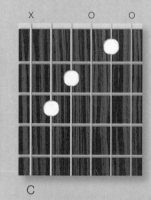

The actual sounding chords produced by this sequence are Badd11 - A - Dadd9 - F♯7.

The **Shubb partial capo** is the most widely available partial capo and is designed to hold down either strings 2, 3 and 4 or strings 3, 4 and 5. The most musical way to get to grips with the possibilities it generates is to examine the properties of these sets of three adjacent strings:

Strings 2, 3, 4 (B, G, D)
Major triad

Strings 3, 4, 5 (G, D, A)
The root notes of a 3-chord trick in D

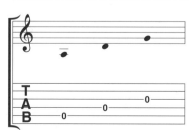

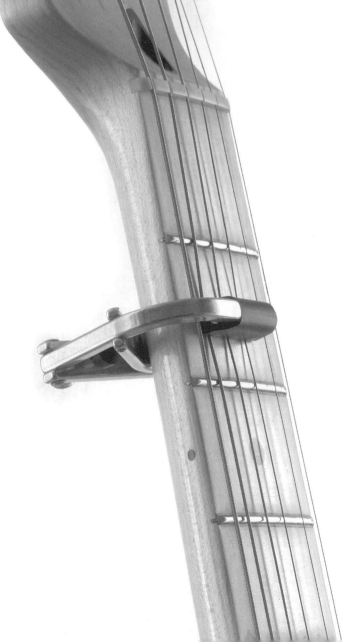

Although not designed for the purpose, with a bit of experimentation it is possible to get the Shubb partial capo to clamp the top or bottom three strings as well. Depending on the width and style of your guitar neck you may find this more or less successful.

Alternatively, if you have a 'Third Hand' capo you can achieve the same effect with ease. If you're lucky enough to be able to do this then you can also experiment with partial capoing on the top three or bottom three strings:

Partial capoing of the top three strings is problematic...

...however, partial capoing of the lower three strings is still effective.

Strings 1, 2, 3 (E, B, G)
Minor triad

Strings 4, 5, 6 (D, A, E)
The root notes of a 3-chord trick in A

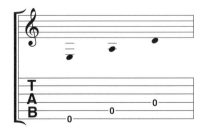

Let's start by finding positions where the partial capo modifies strings so that they are in key with the unclamped, open strings. This can give some very pleasing results. Here's one example for each set of strings. Try these chord shapes and then experiment and create your own voicings.

Strings 2, 3, 4 partial capoed
at the 2nd fret

Partial capo at 2nd fret (strings 2, 3, 4)

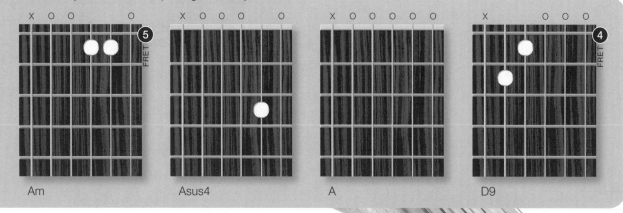

Am   Asus4   A   D9

59

Effective open tuning: E A E A C♯ E (Open A)
Note: on these diagrams fret numbers are measured from the nut, not from the capo.

Strings 3,4,5 partial capoed
at the 2nd fret

Partial capo at 2nd fret (strings 3, 4, 5)

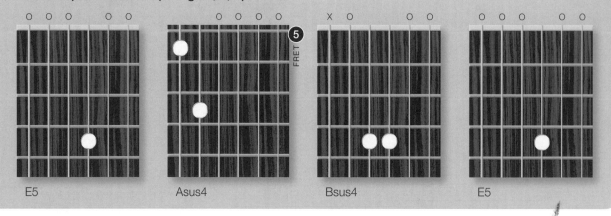

E5   Asus4   Bsus4   E5

60

Effective open tuning: E B E A B E
(D A D G A D tuning, up a tone)

Note: on these diagrams fret numbers are measured from the nut, not from the capo.

And for those who can manage it, here are some examples for the outer sets of strings:

First, an example that mixes fretted notes on the open strings *behind* the capo with more conventional voicings above it!

Partial capo at 5th fret (strings 1, 2, 3)

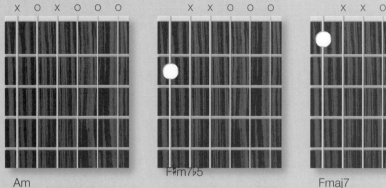

Am   F#m7b5   Fmaj7   E7

61

Again, remember that these diagrams use fret numbers measured from the nut, not from the capo.

This capo position can also be used to play a classic descending chromatic sequence below an A minor chord, as demonstrated below:

62

Partial capo at 5th fret (strings 1, 2, 3)

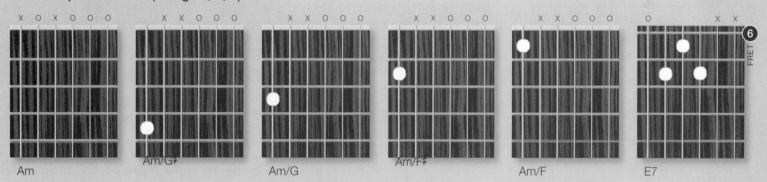

Am   Am/G#   Am/G   Am/F#   Am/F   E7

Partial capo at 7th fret (strings 4, 5, 6)

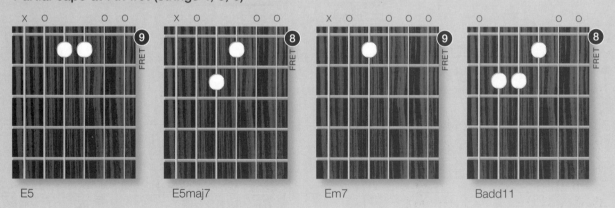

E5   E5maj7   Em7   Badd11

63

Remember when experimenting with partial capoes that any moveable or barre shapes that you already know will still work on the capoed guitar. This effectively means that you have all the benefits of an opening tuning

(exciting new sounds, beautiful ringing open strings etc.) without any of the drawbacks (all your familiar chord shapes will still work).

57

further exploration

Here are some more chord boxes to illustrate what can be done with a partial capo.

These boxes show chords in the key of E major with the capo covering strings 1-3.

Partial capo at 4th fret (strings 1, 2, 3)

Emaj7

F#6/9

G#madd9

Emaj9

B

C#m9

Amaj7/C#

B6

Once again, all fret markings refer to the distance from the nut, not from the capo. So for example, in the Emaj7 shape, the capo is at the fourth fret, and the first fretted note is two frets above that, at the sixth fret on the fourth string.

Watch out for the B6 shape, where the fretting hand is between the capo and the nut!

These boxes show chords in the key of D major with the capo covering strings 2-4. All are between the capo and the nut except for the second Em11 shape.

Try finger-picking these shapes to get the benefit of the tone clusters. Also try playing chords as if there was a standard capo at the VII position. This means you have a capo position that let's you play *either side of it* – a great opportunity to freak out guitarists in your audience!

Partial capo at 7th fret (strings 2, 3, 4)

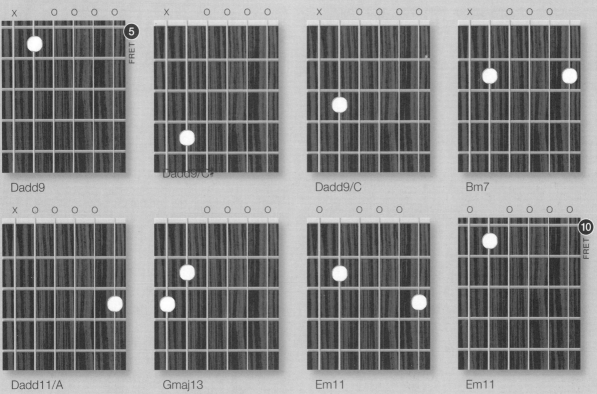

Dadd9 Dadd9/C♯ Dadd9/C Bm7

Dadd11/A Gmaj13 Em11 Em11

These boxes show chords in the key of C major with the capo covering strings 4-6. Try finger-picking these shapes.

Listen out for shapes in which unison notes occur – as in the G6 shape.

Partial capo at 3rd fret (strings 4, 5, 6)

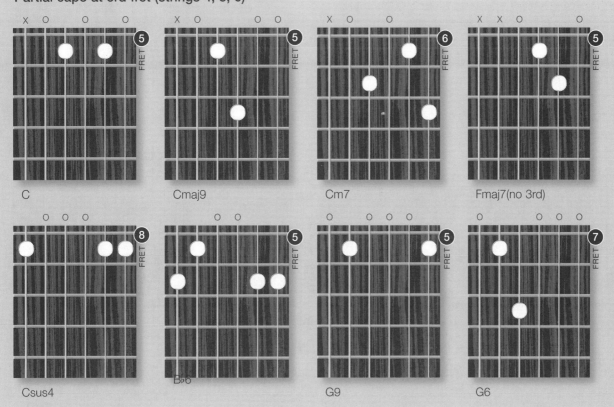

C Cmaj9 Cm7 Fmaj7(no 3rd)

Csus4 B♭6 G9 G6

the third hand capo

The 'Third Hand' capo offers even more flexibility than the partial capo because it allows the clamping of any combination of strings at a given fret. Naturally, therefore, it will allow you to create any of the examples already covered above in the section on partial capos.

Once you have adjusted the individual rubber washers to match the width of the neck and the spacing of the strings at any particular fret, it's simple to clamp any combination of the six strings.

The Third Hand Company's literature helpfully states that there are 63 ways to combine clamped and open notes at any given fret, and that there are therefore 756 possible combinations on the guitar neck. The number of permutations can then be increased further once you start altering the basic tuning of the guitar. At its most basic level The Third Hand capo can be used to help complete beginners hold down effective-sounding chords with just a finger or two, through to more advanced techniques like imitating open tunings (including single-string changes like 'dropped D') and modification of open tunings so they can be switched from major to minor.

Unlike open and altered tunings, none of the notes on the fretboard itself has been changed, because the original pitch of the strings has not been altered. Any barre chord, for example, will still work. This offers a way of avoiding the apparently unavoidable 'drone notes' which open tunings create.

Here's one very simple example of how the Third Hand capo could be used:

A third hand capo at the 2nd fret on the 2nd - 5th strings effectively creates a 'Double Dropped E' tuning: E B E A C♯ E

Third hand capo at 2nd fret (strings 2-5)

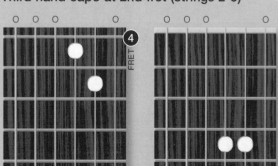

E5   E5maj7   A5/E   Dmaj9

combining capos – the final frontier

For the truly adventurous capo fanatic there are still further possibilities to be explored by combining more than one capo on the neck at a time.

Space doesn't permit an in-depth examination of this fascinating topic here, and in any case, the permutations are almost infinite, so the best advice is just to experiment and see what interesting combinations you can discover.

To start you off on this voyage of musical discovery, here are a few ideas:

1. Combining partial capos and full capos
Remember that any effect that you've created using a partial capo can then be transposed to any key using an additional full capo!

For example, our previous example of strings 2, 3, 4 partial capoed at the 2nd fret to create an effective open A tuning, could be repeated like this to create an open B tuning:

Full capo at 2nd fret
Partial capo on strings 2, 3, 4 at 4th fret.
Effective tuning: F♯ B F♯ B D♯ F♯ (Open B)

2. Combining multiple partial capos
For some truly incredible effects, try combining more than one partial capo.

For example, you could try
Partial capo on strings 3, 4, 5 at 2nd fret
Partial capo on strings 1, 2, 3 at 4th fret
Effective tuning: E B E B D♯ G♯ (Open Emaj7)

or
Partial capo on strings 4, 5, 6 at 7th fret
Particle capo on strings 3, 4, 5 at 9th fret
Effective tuning: B F♯ B E B E (Open Bsus4)

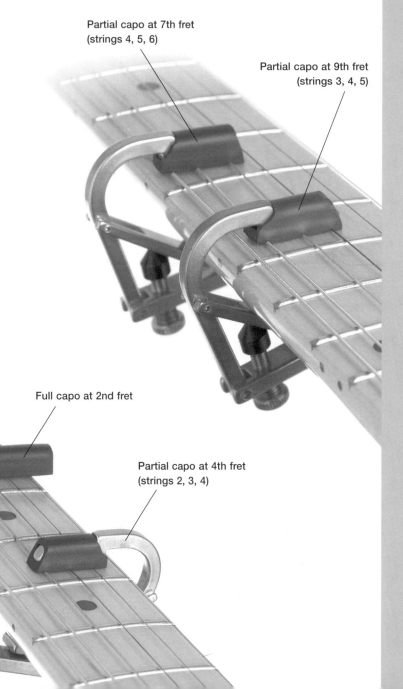

Partial capo at 7th fret
(strings 4, 5, 6)

Partial capo at 9th fret
(strings 3, 4, 5)

Full capo at 2nd fret

Partial capo at 4th fret
(strings 2, 3, 4)

3. Combining multiple third hand capos

The possibilities here are literally infinite, with the only limiting factor being your finances! In fact, with six Third Hand capos you can individually adjust the tuning of every single string on the guitar, creating, by my reckoning, nearly 3 million possible permutations!

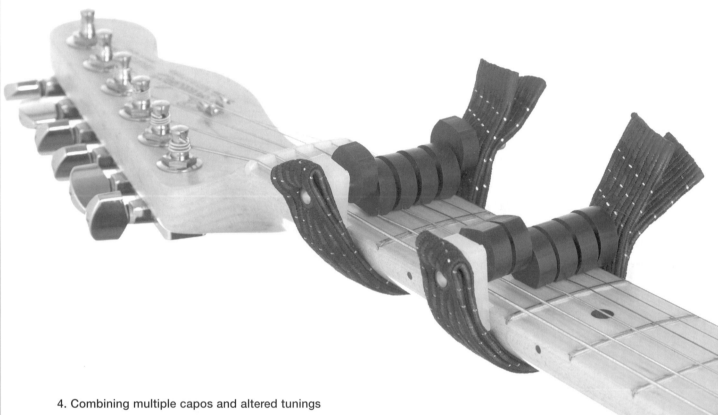

4. Combining multiple capos and altered tunings

The Holy Grail of Capo-philes the world over! This is only recommended for guitarists who are prepared to take a trip into the unknown…

The American guitarist David Willcox combines partial capos with full capos and alternate tunings. He told Acoustic Guitar magazine in November 1994, the idea came from "watching Richie Havens and the way he would fret those beautiful chords over the top of the neck and let the unwound strings ring. I figured I could get a capo to do that, and I could play on top of it. The goal, for me, was to get piano chords – chords that have close clusters. I like having a nice little roll in the middle of the chord to get sounds that you don't ordinarily hear on a guitar. With capos that are cut, you can have strings that are a half step apart right next to each other and get that nice little added ninth roll or suspended fourth."

For his song 'Chet Baker's Unsung Swan Song' (on the album *Home Again*) he used the tuning C G D G A D with a capo covering strings 1-5 at the fifth fret.

"I really love the sound of a guitar that is capoed way up, but without a bass player you've got to have a bottom end. That tuning is an example of me trying to change where you hear the guitar in your ear. If I can capo it way up and have a bass string way low, I can maybe have a guitar sound that comes into your ear and lands in a totally different place."

famous songs that use capos

THE BEATLES

Fret	Title	Capo key	Actual pitch
I	**Hey Jude**	E	F
	I'm Looking Through You	G	A♭
	Ob-la-di, Ob-la-da	A	B♭
	Revolution	A	B♭
	She Said She Said	A	B♭
	Strawberry Fields Forever	A	B♭
	The Inner Light	D	E♭
	The Long and Winding Road	D	E♭
	When I'm Sixty-Four	C	D♭
	Within You Without You	C	D♭
	You'll Be Mine	A	B♭
II	**And Your Bird Can Sing**	D	E
	For No-One	A	B
	Julia	C	D
	Norwegian Wood	D	E
	Nowhere Man	D	E
	Wait	Em	F♯m
III	**Long, Long, Long**	D	F
	Martha My Dear	C	E♭
IV	**Octopus' Garden**	C	E
V	**For You Blue**	A	D
	It's Only Love	G	C
	Michelle	C	F
VII	**Here Comes The Sun**	D	G
VIII	**Girl**	G	D

OTHER ARTISTS

Fret	Artist	Title	Capo key	Actual pitch
I	**Leonard Cohen**	**First We Take Manhattan**	C	C♯
	Bob Marley	No Woman No Cry	C	C♯
	Bryan Adams	Everything I Do	C	C♯
	Simon and Garfunkel	April Come She Will	G	G♯
	Paul Simon	Slip Sliding Away	G	G♯
	Paul Simon	The Obvious Child	G	G♯
	David Bowie	Oh You Pretty Things	F	F♯
	David Bowie	Let's Dance	A	B♭
	David Bowie	Ashes To Ashes	G	G♯
	Kate Bush	Wuthering Heights	C	C♯
	Kate Bush	Babooshka	Dm	D♯m
	Madness	Embarassment	D	D♯
	Abba	The Winner Takes It All	C	C♯
	Moody Blues	Go Now	G	G♯
	John Lennon	Give Peace A Chance	C	C♯
	David Gray	Babylon	D	D♯
	David Gray	Sail Away	Bm	Cm
	Elvis Presley	In The Ghetto	A	B♭
II	**Sting**	**Shape Of My Heart**	Em	F♯m
	Paul Weller	Wild Wood	Am	Bm
	Oasis	Wonderwall	Em	F♯m
	Bryan Adams	Run To You	Em	F♯m
	Simon and Garfunkel	Mrs Robinson	G	A
III	**James Taylor**	**Fire and Rain**	A	C
	James Taylor	You've Got A Friend	G	B♭
	Simon and Garfunkel	Homeward Bound	G	B♭
	Simon and Garfunkel	America	C	B♭
	Radiohead	No Surprises	D	E♭
	Bob Dylan	I Want You	D	F
IV	**Simon and Garfunkel**	**Bookends**	C	E
	Bob Dylan	All Along The Watchtower	Am	C♯m
V	**Buddy Holly**	**That'll Be The Day**	E	A
VI	**Simon and Garfunkel**	**The Sound Of Silence**	Am	E♭m
VII	**The Eagles**	**Hotel California**	Em	Bm
	Travis	Driftwood	D	A
	Simon and Garfunkel	Scarborough Fair	Am	Em
	Bob Dylan	Blowin' In The Wind	G	D

HAL LEONARD PRESENTS

Guitar Cards
Chord Starter Pack

This unique card deck features full-color chord diagrams along with related chords and suggested chord sequences for each. Over 50 essential chords in all! The cards fit easily into guitar cases or pockets, so musicians and songwriters can carry them anywhere. Also great to use as flash cards! 2-1/4" x 3-1/2"

HL00695760 . . . . .Only $5.95!

Price and availability
subject to change
without notice.

FOR MORE INFORMATION,
SEE YOUR LOCAL MUSIC DEALER,
OR WRITE TO:

HAL•LEONARD®
CORPORATION
7777 W. BLUEMOUND RD. P.O. BOX 13819
MILWAUKEE, WISCONSIN 53213

Visit Hal Leonard Online at
www.halleonard.com